# BOOK OF SUPPLEMENTS

# Book of Supplements

## FUNCTIONS, USES, HEALTH BENEFITS

Destinee
Wesley

# Contents

*For those who dream and work hard to accomplish their dreams. And for those who make healthy choices in life. This educational instrument is for you!*

"The first wealth is health" -Ralph Waldo Emerson

"Health is a state of complete harmony of the body, mind, and spirit." — B.K.S. Iyengar

"Nurturing yourself is not selfish – it's essential to your survival and your well-being." – Renee Peterson Trudeau

# TOPICS

# HEALTH BENEFITS OF VITAMINS

<u>Introduction/ Purpose of this Book</u>

Welcome to the "Book of Supplements," your comprehensive guide to understanding the world of dietary supplements and their vital role in promoting health and well-being. In today's fast-paced world, maintaining optimal health can be a challenge. Our diets often lack essential nutrients due to busy lifestyles, processed foods, and environmental factors.

Supplements can bridge these nutritional gaps, providing our bodies with the necessary vitamins, minerals, and other beneficial compounds to function at their best.

This book aims to demystify supplements, offering clear and concise information on a wide range of products. Whether you're seeking to boost your immune system, improve your skin health, enhance mental clarity, or support overall wellness, you'll find valuable insights and practical advice here.

We begin by exploring the fundamental concepts of supplements: what they are, how they work, and why they are important. From there, we delve into detailed descriptions of essential vitamins, vital minerals, potent herbs, and specialized supplements, highlighting their health benefits, sources, and recommended uses.

Each chapter is designed to provide you with evidence-based information, helping you make informed decisions about incorporating supplements into your daily routine. By understanding the specific benefits and appropriate dosages, you can tailor your supplement regimen to meet your individual health needs and goals.

Whether you are new to supplements or looking to deepen your knowledge, "Book of Supplements" is your trusted resource for navigating the diverse and often overwhelming world of dietary supplements. Let this guide empower you to take charge of your health, enhancing your well-being and enriching your life.

We invite you to explore the transformative potential of supplements and embark on a journey towards a healthier, more vibrant you.

## THE IMPORTANCE OF SUPPLEMENTS IN HEALTH AND WELLNESS

In our quest for optimal health and wellness, dietary supplements play a crucial role in bridging nutritional gaps and supporting overall well-being. While a balanced diet should

ideally provide all the nutrients our bodies need, various factors can make it challenging to obtain sufficient vitamins, minerals, and other essential compounds from food alone. This is where supplements come in, offering targeted nutrition to enhance our health.

Nutrient Deficiencies:

Even with the best intentions, many people struggle to meet their daily nutritional requirements. Modern agricultural practices, soil depletion, and food processing can reduce

the nutrient content of the foods we eat. Additionally, lifestyle factors such as stress, lack of sleep, and environmental toxins can increase our nutritional needs. Supplements can help address these deficiencies, ensuring our bodies get the nutrients they need to function properly.

Support for Specific Health Conditions:

Supplements can provide targeted support for specific health conditions. For example, omega-3 fatty acids are known for their heart health benefits, while calcium and vitamin D are essential for bone health. Probiotics support gut health, and antioxidants like vitamin C and E protect against oxidative stress. By addressing particular health concerns with appropriate supplements, individuals can enhance their quality of life and prevent potential health issues.

Enhancing Physical and Mental Performance:

Supplements are also popular among athletes and those looking to boost their physical and mental performance. Protein powders, creatine, and branched-chain amino acids (BCAAs) can support muscle growth and recovery. Nootropics, or cognitive enhancers, such as ginkgo biloba and L-theanine, can improve mental clarity, focus, and cognitive function. These supplements help individuals achieve their fitness and mental goals more effectively.

Aging and Longevity:

As we age, our nutritional needs change, and our bodies may not absorb nutrients as efficiently as they once did. Supplements can help mitigate the effects of aging by providing essential nutrients that support healthy aging and longevity. For instance, coenzyme Q10 (CoQ10) supports cellular energy production and cardiovascular health, while supplements like glucosamine and chondroitin can promote joint health.

Convenience and Accessibility:

In today's busy world, convenience is key. Supplements offer an easy and accessible way to ensure we get the necessary nutrients without extensive meal planning or preparation. They are particularly beneficial for individuals with dietary restrictions, such as vegans or those with food allergies, who may find it challenging to obtain certain nutrients from their diet alone.

Personalized Nutrition:

With advancements in nutritional science, personalized supplementation is becoming increasingly popular. By understanding individual health profiles, genetic predispositions, and specific nutritional needs, tailored supplement plans can be developed to optimize health outcomes. This personalized approach ensures that each person receives the right nutrients in the right amounts for their unique body.

Conclusion:

The importance of supplements in health and wellness cannot be overstated. They offer a practical and effective solution to enhance our diets, support specific health conditions, and promote overall well-being. However, it's crucial to use supplements wisely and in conjunction with a balanced diet and healthy lifestyle. Consulting with healthcare professionals can help ensure that supplement use is safe and beneficial, tailored to individual health needs and goals.

In summary, supplements are a valuable tool in our health and wellness arsenal, helping us achieve and maintain optimal health in a modern world full of nutritional challenges.

# 1

# Understanding Supplements

## Chapter 1: Understanding Supplements

### Definition of Supplements

Dietary supplements are products intended to augment the diet and provide nutrients that may be missing or insufficient in a person's regular food intake. They are designed to deliver vitamins, minerals, amino acids, enzymes, herbs, and other beneficial compounds in a concentrated form. Supplements come in various formats, including tablets, capsules, powders, liquids, and gummies, making them convenient to incorporate into daily routines.

<u>Key Points</u>

Purpose: Supplements aim to fill nutritional gaps, support overall health, and address specific health concerns or conditions.

Composition: They can contain a single nutrient (e.g., vitamin C) or a combination of various nutrients and other beneficial ingredients.

Forms: Available in multiple forms such as pills, powders, liquids, and gummies to suit individual preferences and needs.

Regulation: In many countries, supplements are regulated as food products, not drugs, meaning they must be safe for consumption but do not undergo the same rigorous testing as pharmaceuticals. Examples of Supplements: Vitamins: Vitamin D, vitamin B12, and vitamin E. Minerals: Calcium, magnesium, and iron. Herbs and Botanicals: Echinacea, ginseng, and turmeric. Other Compounds: Omega-3 fatty acids, probiotics, and amino acids like L-arginine.

Overall, supplements play a significant role in supporting dietary needs, promoting health, and enhancing well-being, particularly when dietary intake may be inadequate or specific health conditions require additional nutritional support.

Types of Supplements: (Vitamin, Minerals, Herbs etc.)

Vitamins are organic compounds that are essential for various bodily functions and overall health. They are categorized into two types: water-soluble and fat-soluble vitamins.

**Water-Soluble Vitamins:**

Vitamin C (Ascorbic Acid): Supports the immune system, skin health, and collagen formation.

B Vitamins: Include B1 (Thiamine), B2 (Riboflavin), B3 (Niacin), B5 (Pantothenic Acid), B6 (Pyridoxine), B7 (Biotin), B9 (Folate), and B12 (Cobalamin). These vitamins play crucial roles in energy production, brain function, and cell metabolism.

**Fat-Soluble Vitamins:**

Vitamin A: Important for vision, immune function, and skin health.

Vitamin D: Supports bone health and immune function.

Vitamin E: Acts as an antioxidant, protecting cells from damage.

Vitamin K: Essential for blood clotting and bone health.

1. Minerals:

   Minerals are inorganic elements that are vital for the proper functioning of the body. They are

   divided into two categories: macrominerals and trace minerals.

   Macrominerals:

   Calcium: Crucial for bone and teeth health, muscle function, and nerve signaling.

   Magnesium: Supports muscle and nerve function, blood glucose control, and bone health.

   Potassium: Important for fluid balance, muscle contractions, and nerve signals.

   Sodium: Essential for fluid balance, nerve transmission, and muscle function.

   Trace Minerals:

   Iron: Vital for the production of hemoglobin and oxygen transport in the blood.

   Zinc: Supports immune function, wound healing, and DNA synthesis.

   Selenium: Acts as an antioxidant and supports thyroid function.

   Copper: Essential for iron metabolism and the formation of red blood cells.

2. Herbs and Botanicals:

   Herbal supplements are derived from plants and are used for their therapeutic properties. They can come in various forms, including extracts, teas, powders, and capsules.

Echinacea: Used to boost the immune system and reduce the duration of colds.

Turmeric (Curcumin): Known for its anti-inflammatory and antioxidant properties.

Ginseng: Enhances energy, reduces stress, and improves cognitive function.

Garlic: Supports cardiovascular health and has antimicrobial properties.

Green Tea Extract: Rich in antioxidants, it supports weight loss and cardiovascular health.

3. Amino Acids:

Amino acids are the building blocks of proteins and play a crucial role in many physiological processes.

Essential Amino Acids: Cannot be synthesized by the body and must be obtained from the diet. Examples include leucine, isoleucine, and valine (branched-chain amino acids or BCAAs), lysine, and methionine.

Non-Essential Amino Acids: Can be synthesized by the body. Examples include glutamine, arginine, and alanine.

4. Omega-3 Fatty Acids:

Omega-3 fatty acids are essential fats that have numerous health benefits, particularly for heart and brain health.

EPA (Eicosapentaenoic Acid) and DHA (Docosahexaenoic Acid): Found in fish oil and support cardiovascular health, reduce inflammation, and promote brain function.

ALA (Alpha-Linolenic Acid): Found in flaxseed, chia seeds, and walnuts, and can be converted into EPA and DHA in the body, though less efficiently.

5. Probiotics:

Probiotics are live bacteria and yeasts that are beneficial for gut health. They help maintain a healthy balance of gut flora, support digestion, and boost the immune system.

Lactobacillus: Commonly found in yogurt and fermented foods, helps with digestion and prevents diarrhea.

Bifidobacterium: Found in some dairy products, supports immune function and gut health.

Saccharomyces Boulardii: A yeast that helps treat and prevent diarrhea and other digestive disorders.

6. Specialized Supplements: These include a variety of compounds that provide specific health benefits.

Coenzyme Q10 (CoQ10): Supports cellular energy production and heart health.

Melatonin: A hormone that regulates sleep-wake cycles, commonly used as a sleep aid.

L-Theanine: An amino acid found in tea that promotes relaxation without drowsiness.

Each type of supplement serves a specific purpose and can be used to address particular health needs. However, it's important to use supplements wisely and consult with a healthcare professional to ensure they are appropriate for your individual health situation and goals.

How Supplements Work In the Body :

Absorption and Metabolism:

Digestive Process: When you consume a supplement, it first enters the digestive system. Here, it is broken down into its component nutrients. The process begins in the stomach, where stomach acids and enzymes start breaking down the supplement. The majority of nutrient absorption happens in the small intestine.

Bioavailability: The term bioavailability refers to the proportion of a nutrient that is absorbed and utilized by the body. Factors such as the supplement's form (e.g., pill, liquid, powder), the presence of other nutrients, and individual digestive health can influence bioavailability.

Transport and Distribution:

Bloodstream: Once the nutrients from supplements are absorbed into the bloodstream through the walls of the small intestine, they are transported to various tissues and organs. Water-soluble nutrients, like most B vitamins and vitamin C, dissolve in blood plasma and are readily transported. Fat-soluble vitamins (A, D, E, and K) are often transported with the help of lipoproteins.

Storage: The body can store certain nutrients for later use. Fat-soluble vitamins are stored in the liver and adipose tissues, while water-soluble vitamins generally have limited storage and need to be replenished regularly.

Utilization:

Structural Functions: Some nutrients contribute to the structural components of the body. Calcium, for example, is essential for bone and teeth formation, while collagen (formed with the help of vitamin C) is crucial for healthy skin, tendons, and ligaments.

Regulatory Functions: Certain supplements help regulate bodily processes. Omega-3 fatty acids, for instance, are involved in anti-inflammatory responses, and vitamin D helps regulate calcium and phosphate balance in the body.

Excretion:

**Specific Functions of Common Supplements:**

Vitamin A: Once absorbed, vitamin A supports vision by being a component of the protein rhodopsin, which allows the eyes to see in low light conditions. It also supports immune function by maintaining the health of skin and mucous membranes.

Calcium: Essential for bone health, calcium works by being deposited in the bone matrix.

It is also crucial for muscle contraction, nerve signaling, and blood clotting.

Individual Variability:

Dietary Interactions: The presence of other nutrients and compounds in your diet can influence the absorption and effectiveness of supplements. For example, vitamin C enhances iron absorption, while excessive calcium can interfere with magnesium and zinc absorption.

## Conclusion

Supplements work by providing essential nutrients that support the body's biochemical processes, structural integrity, and regulatory functions. They are absorbed, transported, utilized, and excreted in ways that complement the body's natural processes. Understanding these mechanisms can help you make informed decisions about which supplements to take and how to use them effectively to support your health and wellness goals. Always consult with a healthcare professional before starting any new supplement regimen to ensure it's appropriate for your individual needs.

HEALTH

# Essential Vitamins

## Chapter 2: Essential Vitamins

**Vitamin A**

Sources of Vitamin A:

Animal Sources: Liver, fish liver oils (such as cod liver oil), egg yolks, butter, cheese, and whole milk.

Plant Sources: Fruits and vegetables rich in beta-carotene, a precursor to vitamin A. Examples include carrots, sweet potatoes, spinach, kale, apricots, and mangoes.

Health Benefits of Vitamin A:

Vision Support: Vitamin A is essential for maintaining good vision, especially in low light conditions. It helps form visual pigments in the retina, aiding in night vision and overall eye health.

Immune Function: Vitamin A plays a crucial role in supporting the immune system by helping maintain the integrity of mucosal surfaces, such as the lining of the respiratory, gastrointestinal, and urinary tracts, which act as barriers against pathogens.

Skin Health: It supports healthy skin by promoting cell turnover and wound healing. Vitamin A is often used in skincare products for its anti-aging and acne-fighting properties.

Reproductive Health: Vitamin A is important for normal reproductive processes and fetal development during pregnancy.

Bone Health: It contributes to bone growth and remodeling, helping maintain bone density and strength.

<u>Uses of Vitamin A Supplement:</u>

Prevention and Treatment of Vitamin A Deficiency: In cases where dietary intake of vitamin A is inadequate, supplements can help prevent or treat deficiency-related conditions, such as night blindness, dry eyes, and increased susceptibility to infections.

Supporting Eye Health: Vitamin A supplements may be prescribed for individuals with certain eye conditions, such as retinitis pigmentosa or age-related macular degeneration, to support overall eye health and function.

Skin Conditions: Topical vitamin A derivatives, such as retinoids, are used in skincare products to treat acne, reduce wrinkles, and improve skin texture and tone.

Immune Support: In certain situations, such as during illness or recovery from surgery, vitamin A supplements may be recommended to support immune function and promote healing.

It's important to note that while vitamin A is essential for health, excessive intake can be harmful. Always consult with a healthcare professional before starting any supplement regimen, especially if you have existing health conditions or are pregnant or breastfeeding.

**Vitamin B Complex:**

Vitamin B complex refers to a group of eight essential B vitamins that play crucial roles in maintaining good health and well-being. Each of these vitamins contributes to the body's energy production and various metabolic processes. Here is an overview of the functions, sources, and health benefits of the B vitamins.

## *Functions of B Vitamins*

1. Vitamin B1 (Thiamine):

   Functions: Converts carbohydrates into energy, essential for glucose metabolism, supports nerve, muscle, and heart function.

   Sources: Whole grains, pork, fish, legumes, seeds, nuts.

2. Vitamin B2 (Riboflavin):

   Functions: Plays a key role in energy production, helps break down fats, drugs, and steroid hormones, maintains healthy skin and eyes.

   Sources: Eggs, organ meats, lean meats, milk, green vegetables, fortified cereals.

3. Vitamin B3 (Niacin):

   Functions: Converts nutrients into energy, involved in DNA repair, produces stress and sex hormones, improves circulation.

   Sources: Poultry, beef, fish, whole grains, peanuts, legumes.

4. Vitamin B5 (Pantothenic Acid):

   Functions: Essential for the synthesis of coenzyme A, important in fatty acid metabolism, synthesizes and metabolizes proteins, carbohydrates, and fats.

   Sources: Chicken, beef, potatoes, oats, tomatoes, whole grains, egg yolk.

5. Vitamin B6 (Pyridoxine):

   Functions: Involved in amino acid metabolism, red blood cell production, neurotransmitter synthesis.

   Sources: Poultry, fish, potatoes, chickpeas, bananas, fortified cereals.

6. Vitamin B7 (Biotin):

   Functions: Plays a role in the metabolism of fats, carbohydrates, and proteins, important for healthy skin, hair, and nails.

   Sources: Eggs, almonds, spinach, sweet potatoes, cheese, whole grains.

7. Vitamin B9 (Folate/Folic Acid):

   Functions: Vital for DNA synthesis and repair, crucial for cell division and growth, especially important during pregnancy for fetal development.

Sources: Leafy green vegetables, legumes, seeds, liver, fortified grains.

8. Vitamin B12 (Cobalamin):

Functions: Necessary for red blood cell formation, neurological function, and DNA synthesis.

Sources: Meat, fish, dairy products, eggs, fortified cereals.

## Health Benefits

Brain Function: B vitamins, especially B6, B9, and B12, are crucial for brain health, cognitive function, and reducing the risk of neuro-degenerative diseases.

Cell Metabolism: They play key roles in cell metabolism and the synthesis of new cells.

## Summary

The vitamin B complex is vital for overall health, affecting energy levels, brain function, and cellular processes. Ensuring an adequate intake through a balanced diet rich in various

sources of these vitamins is crucial for maintaining optimal health.

**Vitamin C (Ascorbic Acid):**

Vitamin C, also known as ascorbic acid, is a water-soluble vitamin essential for many bodily functions. It is a powerful antioxidant that supports overall health and plays a crucial role in various physiological processes.

**Sources of Vitamin C**

Vitamin C is found in a wide variety of fruits and vegetables. Some of the richest sources include:

Citrus Fruits: Oranges, lemons, limes, grapefruits

Berries: Strawberries, raspberries, blueberries, blackberries

Tropical Fruits: Kiwi, mango, papaya, pineapple

Vegetables: Bell peppers, broccoli, Brussels sprouts, cauliflower, spinach, kale, tomatoes

Other Sources: Potatoes, sweet potatoes, cantaloupe, watermelon

**Functions of Vitamin C**

Vitamin C plays several vital roles in the body, including: Antioxidant Protection. Protects cells from damage caused by free radicals and oxidative stress.

1. Collagen Synthesis: Essential for the production of collagen, a protein that helps maintain healthy skin, blood vessels, bones, and cartilage.
2. Immune Function: Enhances the immune system by supporting various cellular functions, stimulating the production and function of white blood cells.
3. Wound Healing: Promotes the healing of wounds and repair of tissues.
4. Iron Absorption: Improves the absorption of non-heme iron (iron from plant-based foods), which is important for preventing iron deficiency anemia.
5. Neurotransmitter Synthesis: Involved in the synthesis of neurotransmitters, which are essential for brain function and mood regulation.
6. Reducing the Risk of Chronic Diseases: Its antioxidant properties help reduce the risk of chronic diseases such as heart disease and cancer.

**Health Benefits of Vitamin C**

1. Boosts Immunity: Enhances the immune system, making it more effective at fighting infections and reducing the severity and duration of colds.

2. Protects Against Cardiovascular Disease: Helps lower blood pressure, reduce LDL cholesterol and triglycerides, and improve endothelial function, thus protecting against heart disease.
3. Promotes Healthy Skin: Aids in collagen production, which keeps skin firm and healthy, and helps reduce wrinkles and other signs of aging.
4. Prevents Iron Deficiency: Enhances the absorption of iron from plant-based foods, helping to prevent anemia.
5. Supports Eye Health: May reduce the risk of cataracts and age-related macular degeneration due to its antioxidant properties.
6. May Reduce Cancer Risk: High intake of fruits and vegetables rich in vitamin C is associated with a lower risk of various types of cancer due to its role in protecting cells from oxidative damage.
7. Aids in Wound Healing: Necessary for the growth, development, and repair of all body tissues, vitamin C plays a critical role in wound healing and the maintenance of healthy bones and teeth.

### Summary

Vitamin C is an essential nutrient that supports many critical functions in the body, including antioxidant protection, collagen synthesis, immune function, and the absorption of iron.

Consuming a diet rich in fruits and vegetables can help ensure adequate vitamin C intake, which is vital for overall health and the prevention of various diseases.

## *Vitamin D:*

Vitamin D is a fat-soluble vitamin essential for maintaining several critical bodily functions. It is unique because it can be synthesized in the skin upon exposure to sunlight. It exists in two main forms: D2 (ergocalciferol) and D3 (cholecalciferol).

## Functions of Vitamin D

1. Calcium Absorption: Facilitates the absorption of calcium in the intestines, which is crucial for the formation and maintenance of healthy bones and teeth.
2. Bone Health: Works with calcium and phosphorus to promote bone mineralization and prevent disorders like rickets in children and osteomalacia or osteoporosis in adults.
3. Immune System Support: Modulates the immune system, enhancing the body's defense against infections.
4. Muscle Function: Essential for muscle function and strength.
5. Cell Growth and Differentiation: Plays a role in cell growth and differentiation, impacting overall cellular health.

## Sources of Vitamin D

Vitamin D can be obtained from various sources:

1. Sunlight: The body synthesizes vitamin D3 when the skin is exposed to UVB rays from sunlight. About 10-30 minutes of midday sun exposure several times a week is usually sufficient, depending on skin type, location, and season.
2. Food Sources:
   Fatty Fish: Salmon, mackerel, sardines, and tuna
   Fish Liver Oils: Cod liver oil
   Fortified Foods: Milk, orange juice, cereals, and plant-based milk alternatives
   Egg Yolks: Contain small amounts of vitamin D
   Beef Liver: Another source of vitamin D

3. Supplements: Available as vitamin D2 (ergocalciferol) and D3 (cholecalciferol). Vitamin D3 is generally more effective at raising blood levels of vitamin D.

## Health Benefits of Vitamin D

1. Bone and Teeth Health: Prevents bone disorders like rickets, osteomalacia, and osteoporosis by ensuring proper calcium absorption and bone mineralization.
2. Immune Function: Enhances the pathogen-fighting effects of monocytes and macrophages — white blood cells that are important parts of your immune defense — and decreases inflammation.
3. Reduced Risk of Chronic Diseases: Linked to a lower risk of multiple sclerosis, heart disease, and certain types of cancer.
4. Mood Regulation: May help regulate mood and ward off depression. Some studies have found a link between vitamin D deficiency and depression.
5. Weight Management: There is some evidence to suggest that vitamin D might help in weight loss or maintaining a healthy weight.
6. Muscle Function: Adequate levels of vitamin D help maintain muscle strength and reduce the risk of falls in older adults.

## Summary

Vitamin D is vital for maintaining healthy bones and teeth, supporting the immune system, brain, and nervous system, and regulating insulin levels. It can be obtained from sunlight exposure, certain foods, and supplements. Adequate intake of vitamin D is essential for overall health and the prevention of several chronic diseases.

## *Vitamin E:*

Vitamin E is a fat-soluble nutrient that acts as a powerful anti-oxidant, helping to protect cells from damage caused by free radicals. It encompasses a group of compounds that include tocopherols and tocotrienols.

## *Functions of Vitamin E*

1. Antioxidant Protection: Neutralizes free radicals, which can damage cells and contribute to aging and various diseases.
2. Immune Function: Enhances immune response and protects against infections by
promoting the production of immune cells.
3. Skin Health: Supports skin health by reducing oxidative stress and maintaining skin integrity.
4. Anti-Inflammatory Properties: Helps reduce inflammation in the body.
5. Gene Expression: Plays a role in gene expression and regulation.
6. Blood Vessel Health: Prevents the oxidation of LDL cholesterol, which can lead to atherosclerosis, and supports healthy blood vessel function.

## *Sources of Vitamin E*

Vitamin E is found in a variety of foods, particularly those high in fat. Some of the richest sources include:

1. Nuts and Seeds: Almonds, sunflower seeds, hazelnuts, and pine nuts.
2. Vegetable Oils: Sunflower oil, safflower oil, wheat germ oil, and olive oil.
3. Green Leafy Vegetables: Spinach, broccoli, and Swiss chard.
4. Fruits: Avocados, kiwi, and mango.

5. Fortified Foods: Some breakfast cereals and margarines are fortified with vitamin E.
6. Other Sources: Eggs and fatty fish like salmon and trout.

## *Health Benefits of Vitamin E*

1. Protects Against Oxidative Stress: Helps protect cells from damage caused by free radicals, reducing the risk of chronic diseases such as heart disease and cancer.
2. Supports Skin Health: Promotes healthy skin by reducing UV damage and improving skin moisture and elasticity. It's often used in skincare products to treat conditions like eczema and psoriasis.
3. Boosts Immune Function: Enhances the body's immune response, particularly important for elderly individuals whose immune function naturally declines with age.
4. Reduces Inflammation: Acts as an anti-inflammatory agent, which can help reduce symptoms of inflammatory conditions like arthritis.
5. Improves Eye Health: May help reduce the risk of age-related macular degeneration (AMD) and cataracts.
6. Cardiovascular Health: Prevents the oxidation of LDL cholesterol, which can help reduce the risk of atherosclerosis and other cardiovascular diseases.
7. Cognitive Health: May contribute to improved cognitive function and reduced risk of neurodegenerative diseases like Alzheimer's.

## *Summary*

Vitamin E is a crucial antioxidant that protects cells from damage, supports immune function, and promotes skin and eye health. Obtaining adequate amounts of vitamin E from a balanced diet rich in nuts, seeds, vegetable oils, and green leafy vegetables is essential for overall well- being and the prevention of various chronic diseases.

## Vitamin K:

Vitamin K is a fat-soluble vitamin essential for various bodily functions, primarily involved in blood clotting and bone health. It exists in two main forms: K1 (phylloquinone) and K2 (menaquinone).

## Functions of Vitamin K

1. Blood Clotting: Essential for the synthesis of proteins required for blood coagulation, helping to prevent excessive bleeding.
2. Bone Health: Involved in the regulation of bone metabolism, promoting the binding of calcium to the bone matrix and reducing the risk of osteoporosis.
3. Heart Health: Helps prevent arterial calcification, reducing the risk of cardiovascular
   diseases by regulating calcium deposition.
4. Cell Growth and Health: Plays a role in regulating cell growth and maintaining healthy tissues.

## Sources of Vitamin K

Vitamin K can be obtained from various dietary sources, particularly green leafy vegetables and fermented foods.

1. Vitamin K1 (Phylloquinone):
   Green Leafy Vegetables: Kale, spinach, broccoli, Brussels sprouts, collard greens, and Swiss chard.
   Vegetable Oils: Soybean oil, canola oil, and olive oil.
   Other Vegetables: Asparagus, green beans, and peas.
2. Vitamin K2 (Menaquinone):

Fermented Foods: Natto (fermented soybeans), sauerkraut, and kimchi.

Animal Products: Meat, liver, and dairy products like cheese and egg yolks.

Other Sources: Some fish such as salmon and mackerel.

## *Health Benefits of Vitamin K*

1. Promotes Healthy Blood Clotting: Prevents excessive bleeding by aiding in the production of clotting factors. Essential for people taking anticoagulant medications to maintain a balance.
2. Supports Bone Health: Reduces the risk of fractures and osteoporosis by aiding in the regulation of calcium and promoting bone mineralization.
3. Cardiovascular Health: Prevents the calcification of arteries, contributing to better cardiovascular health and reducing the risk of heart disease.
4. Improves Cognitive Health: Some studies suggest that adequate vitamin K levels may support brain function and reduce the risk of cognitive decline.
5. Reduces the Risk of Cancer: Emerging research indicates that vitamin K might have a role in reducing the risk of certain cancers, though more studies are needed to confirm this.

## *Summary*

Vitamin K is crucial for blood clotting, bone health, and preventing arterial calcification. It can be obtained from green leafy vegetables, fermented foods, and animal products. Ensuring an adequate intake of vitamin K through a balanced diet is essential for maintaining good health and preventing various chronic conditions.

# Vital Minerals

### <u>Chapter 3: Vital Minerals</u>

*Calcium*

Calcium is a vital mineral for many bodily functions and is the most abundant mineral in the human body. It is crucial for maintaining strong bones and teeth, muscle function, and various metabolic processes.

*Functions of Calcium*

1. Bone Health: Provides structural strength to bones and teeth, essential for bone formation and maintenance.
2. Muscle Function: Necessary for muscle contraction and relaxation, including the heart muscle.
3. Nerve Transmission: Plays a key role in transmitting nerve impulses.
4. Blood Clotting: Vital for the blood coagulation process.

5. Cellular Functions: Involved in cellular signaling, hormone secretion, and enzyme function.

## Sources of Calcium

Calcium can be obtained from various dietary sources, including dairy products, plant-based foods, and fortified items.

1. Dairy Products: Milk, cheese, yogurt, and other dairy products are rich sources of calcium.
2. Leafy Green Vegetables: Kale, broccoli, bok choy, and collard greens.
3. Fortified Foods: Fortified plant-based milk (such as almond, soy, and rice milk), fortified orange juice, and fortified cereals.
4. Fish: Sardines and salmon (with bones) are good sources.
5. Nuts and Seeds: Almonds, sesame seeds, and chia seeds.
6. Legumes: Beans and lentils.

## Health Benefits of Calcium

1. Strong Bones and Teeth: Essential for the development and maintenance of healthy bones and teeth, reducing the risk of osteoporosis and fractures.
2. Cardiovascular Health: Helps regulate heart rhythms and may lower blood pressure.
3. Weight Management: Some studies suggest calcium might help with weight management by promoting fat loss.
4. Cancer Prevention: May reduce the risk of certain cancers, including colorectal cancer.
5. Prevention of Kidney Stones: Adequate calcium intake can help reduce the risk of developing kidney stones by binding with oxalates in the digestive tract.

6. PMS Relief: May help alleviate symptoms of premenstrual syndrome (PMS).

## Summary

Calcium is essential for maintaining strong bones and teeth, proper muscle and nerve function, and various metabolic processes. It can be obtained from dairy products, leafy green vegetables, fortified foods, fish, nuts, seeds, and legumes. Ensuring adequate calcium intake is crucial for overall health and the prevention of various conditions, including osteoporosis and cardiovascular diseases.

## Iron:

Iron is an essential mineral crucial for various bodily functions. It is a key component of hemoglobin in red blood cells and myoglobin in muscles, enabling oxygen transport and storage.

## Functions of Iron

1. Oxygen Transport: Iron is a vital part of hemoglobin, the protein in red blood cells that carries oxygen from the lungs to tissues throughout the body.
2. Oxygen Storage: It is also a component of myoglobin, a protein that stores oxygen in muscles.
3. Energy Production: Involved in various metabolic processes, including energy production and DNA synthesis.
4. Immune Function: Supports a healthy immune system by aiding in the production and maturation of immune cells.
5. Cognitive Function: Essential for brain development and function, influencing learning and memory.

6. Enzyme Function: Acts as a cofactor for several enzymes involved in metabolism and other cellular processes.

## Sources of Iron

Iron is available in two forms in the diet: heme iron and non-heme iron.

1. Heme Iron: Found in animal-based foods and is more easily absorbed by the body.
   Red Meat: Beef, lamb, and pork
   Poultry: Chicken and turkey
   Fish and Seafood: Tuna, sardines, and shrimp
   Organ Meats: Liver and kidneys
2. Non-Heme Iron: Found in plant-based foods and fortified foods, less readily absorbed but important for vegetarians and vegans.

Legumes: Lentils, chickpeas, beans, and soybeans
Tofu and Tempeh: Soy-based products
Nuts and Seeds: Pumpkin seeds, sesame seeds, and cashews

## Health Benefits of Iron

1. Prevents Anemia: Adequate iron intake prevents iron-deficiency anemia, characterized by fatigue, weakness, and pale skin.
2. Improves Physical Performance: Sufficient iron levels support optimal muscle function and endurance by ensuring efficient oxygen delivery to muscles.
3. Supports Cognitive Development: Essential for brain development and cognitive function, particularly in infants and young children.

4. Boosts Immune Function: Helps maintain a robust immune system, enhancing the body's
ability to fight infections.
5. Enhances Energy Levels: Prevents fatigue and enhances overall energy levels by supporting cellular energy production.
6. Promotes Healthy Pregnancy: Crucial for fetal development and preventing maternal anemia, reducing the risk of preterm delivery and low birth weight.

## Summary

Iron is essential for oxygen transport, energy production, immune function, and cognitive health. It can be obtained from both animal and plant sources, with heme iron being more readily absorbed than non-heme iron. Ensuring adequate iron intake is crucial for preventing anemia, enhancing physical and cognitive performance, and supporting overall health.

## Magnesium:

Magnesium is an essential mineral involved in over 300 biochemical reactions in the body. It plays a crucial role in various physiological functions, including energy production, muscle and nerve function, and bone health.

## Functions of Magnesium

1. Energy Production: Vital for ATP (adenosine triphosphate) synthesis, the primary energy carrier in cells.
2. Protein Synthesis: Essential for the synthesis of proteins from amino acids.
3. Muscle and Nerve Function: Regulates muscle contractions and nerve signals.

4. Blood Glucose Control: Aids in maintaining healthy blood sugar levels.
5. Blood Pressure Regulation: Helps regulate blood pressure by relaxing blood vessels.
6. Bone Health: Contributes to the structural development of bones and is necessary for the synthesis of DNA and RNA.
7. Electrolyte Balance: Maintains a balance of electrolytes like potassium, calcium, and

sodium.

## Sources of Magnesium

Magnesium can be obtained from a variety of dietary sources, primarily from plant-based foods and whole grains.

1. Nuts and Seeds: Almonds, cashews, pumpkin seeds, and sunflower seeds.
2. Whole Grains: Brown rice, quinoa, oats, and whole wheat.
3. Legumes: Black beans, chickpeas, lentils, and soybeans.
4. Leafy Green Vegetables: Spinach, kale, Swiss chard, and collard greens.
5. Fruits: Avocados, bananas, and dried fruits like figs and raisins.
6. Fish: Salmon, mackerel, and halibut.
7. Dairy Products: Milk and yogurt.
8. Dark Chocolate: High in magnesium content.

## Health Benefits of Magnesium

1. Supports Bone Health: Essential for bone formation, magnesium influences the activity of osteoblasts and osteoclasts, which are cells responsible for bone formation and resorption, respectively.

2. Promotes Heart Health: Helps maintain a normal heart rhythm, supports blood vessel function, and lowers blood pressure, reducing the risk of cardiovascular diseases.

3. Regulates Blood Sugar Levels: Improves insulin sensitivity, which can help manage and prevent type 2 diabetes.

4. Reduces Muscle Cramps and Spasms: Alleviates muscle cramps and spasms by aiding in muscle relaxation and function.

5. Enhances Mood and Reduces Stress: Involved in the regulation of neurotransmitters that affect mood and brain function, potentially reducing symptoms of depression and anxiety.

6. Improves Sleep Quality: Contributes to better sleep quality by regulating neurotransmitters and the hormone melatonin.

7. Anti-Inflammatory Effects: Reduces inflammation markers in the body, potentially lowering the risk of chronic diseases associated with inflammation.

8. Supports Digestive Health: Helps maintain regular bowel movements and prevent constipation by relaxing intestinal muscles.

## *Summary*

Magnesium is vital for numerous bodily functions, including energy production, muscle and nerve function, blood sugar regulation, and bone health. It is found in various foods such as nuts, seeds, whole grains, legumes, leafy green vegetables, fish, dairy products, and dark chocolate. Ensuring adequate magnesium intake is essential for maintaining overall health and preventing various chronic conditions.

## *Zinc:*

Zinc is an essential trace mineral that plays a vital role in numerous aspects of cellular metabolism. It is crucial for immune function, DNA synthesis, protein synthesis, wound healing, and cell division.

## *Functions of Zinc*

1. Immune Function: Vital for the development and function of immune cells. It helps the body fight off invading bacteria and viruses.
2. Protein Synthesis: Necessary for the synthesis of proteins, which are essential for cell growth and repair.
3. DNA Synthesis: Involved in DNA replication and repair.
4. Enzyme Function: Acts as a cofactor for over 300 enzymes, facilitating various biochemical reactions in the body.
5. Wound Healing: Essential for skin health and wound healing, as it helps maintain the integrity of skin and mucous membranes.
6. Growth and Development: Critical for proper growth and development, particularly during pregnancy, childhood, and adolescence.
7. Antioxidant Defense: Plays a role in the antioxidant defense system, protecting cells from damage by free radicals.
8. Taste and Smell: Necessary for the proper functioning of the taste and smell senses.

## *Sources of Zinc*

Zinc is found in a variety of foods, both animal and plant-based.

1. Animal Sources:
Meat: Beef, pork, and lamb

Poultry: Chicken and turkey

Seafood: Oysters (the highest source), crab, lobster, and other shellfish

Dairy Products: Milk, cheese, and yogurt

Eggs: Particularly the yolk

2. Plant Sources:

Legumes: Chickpeas, lentils, and beans

Nuts and Seeds: Pumpkin seeds, sesame seeds, and cashews

Whole Grains: Quinoa, brown rice, oats, and whole wheat

Vegetables: Spinach, kale, and mushrooms

Fortified Foods: Some breakfast cereals and plant-based milk alternatives

## *Health Benefits of Zinc*

1. Boosts Immune System: Enhances the immune system by supporting the function of immune cells and reducing inflammation, helping to protect against infections.
2. Supports Wound Healing: Promotes wound healing by supporting skin integrity and cellular repair processes.
3. Improves Cognitive Function: Essential for brain health and cognitive function, potentially improving memory and learning abilities.
4. Reduces Inflammation: Acts as an anti-inflammatory agent, helping to reduce chronic inflammation linked to various health conditions.
5. Aids in Growth and Development: Crucial for proper physical growth and development during pregnancy, infancy, and childhood.
6. Maintains Healthy Skin: Helps prevent and treat skin conditions like acne by regulating oil production and inflammation.

7. Enhances Fertility: Important for reproductive health, zinc deficiency can lead to impaired fertility in both men and women.
8. Supports Sensory Functions: Necessary for the proper function of taste and smell receptors.

## Summary

Zinc is an essential mineral that supports immune function, protein synthesis, DNA synthesis, wound healing, and growth and development. It is found in a variety of animal and plant- based foods, including meat, seafood, legumes, nuts, seeds, and whole grains. Adequate zinc intake is crucial for maintaining overall health, preventing infections, promoting healthy skin, and supporting cognitive and reproductive health.

## Selenium:

Selenium is an essential trace mineral that plays a critical role in many bodily processes, including metabolism, thyroid function, and protection against oxidative stress. It is a key component of various enzymes and proteins.

## Functions of Selenium

1. Antioxidant Protection: Integral part of antioxidant enzymes like glutathione peroxidases, which help protect cells from damage caused by free radicals.
2. Thyroid Function: Crucial for the production of thyroid hormones and the regulation of thyroid function.
3. Immune System Support: Enhances immune response and helps the body fight off infections.
4. DNA Synthesis and Repair: Involved in the synthesis and repair of DNA.

5. Reproductive Health: Plays a role in sperm motility and may reduce the risk of miscarriage.
6. Anti-inflammatory Effects: Helps reduce inflammation by regulating the production of inflammatory compounds.

## Sources of Selenium

Selenium can be found in a variety of foods, with the content varying depending on the selenium content of the soil where plants are grown or animals are raised.

1. Brazil Nuts: One of the richest sources of selenium.
2. Seafood: Tuna, shrimp, sardines, and salmon.
3. Meat: Beef, pork, chicken, and turkey.
4. Dairy Products: Milk, cheese, and yogurt.
5. Grains and Cereals: Brown rice, whole wheat bread, and oats.
6. Eggs: Particularly the yolk.
7. Legumes: Lentils, beans, and chickpeas.
8. Vegetables: Spinach, broccoli, and mushrooms.

## Health Benefits of Selenium

1. Antioxidant Defense: Protects cells from oxidative damage, reducing the risk of chronic diseases such as heart disease and cancer.
2. Thyroid Health: Supports thyroid hormone metabolism and protects the thyroid gland from damage by oxidative stress.
3. Immune System Enhancement: Boosts immune function and helps fight infections more effectively.
4. Reduced Risk of Cancer: May reduce the risk of certain cancers, including prostate, lung, and colorectal cancer, by protecting cells from oxidative damage and enhancing immune function.

5. Heart Health: Helps reduce inflammation and oxidative stress, which are risk factors for heart disease.
6. Cognitive Health: May protect against cognitive decline and neurodegenerative diseases like Alzheimer's.
7. Reproductive Health: Supports fertility in both men and women, with a particular role in
sperm motility and health.
8. Anti-inflammatory Properties: Reduces inflammation, which can help manage conditions like arthritis and asthma.

## Summary

Selenium is an essential mineral that supports antioxidant defense, thyroid function, immune response, and reproductive health. It can be obtained from a variety of dietary sources, including Brazil nuts, seafood, meat, dairy products, grains, eggs, legumes, and vegetables.

Adequate selenium intake is crucial for overall health, reducing the risk of chronic diseases, and supporting vital bodily functions.

## Potassium:

Potassium is a vital mineral and electrolyte that plays a crucial role in various physiological processes within the body. It is essential for maintaining proper fluid balance, muscle function, nerve transmission, and heart health.

## Functions of Potassium

1. Fluid Balance: Helps regulate fluid balance within cells and tissues, ensuring proper hydration and maintaining normal blood pressure.
2. Muscle Function: Necessary for muscle contraction, including the beating of the heart
and skeletal muscle movement.

3. Nerve Transmission: Facilitates the transmission of nerve impulses, which is essential for communication between nerves and the brain.

4. Heart Health: Supports normal heart rhythm and function, helping to regulate heartbeat and prevent arrhythmias.

5. Blood Pressure Regulation: Helps lower blood pressure by counteracting the effects of
sodium and promoting vasodilation.

6. Kidney Function: Supports kidney function by aiding in the elimination of waste products through urine.

7. Bone Health: Some evidence suggests that potassium may help reduce the risk of osteoporosis by supporting bone mineral density.

## Sources of Potassium

Potassium is found in a wide variety of foods, with fruits, vegetables, and legumes being particularly rich sources. Here are some potassium-rich foods:

1. Fruits: Bananas, oranges, kiwi, apricots, cantaloupe, and strawberries.

2. Vegetables: Potatoes (both white and sweet potatoes), spinach, kale, broccoli, Brussels sprouts, and tomatoes.

3. Legumes: Kidney beans, black beans, lentils, chickpeas, and soybeans.

4. Nuts and Seeds: Almonds, pistachios, sunflower seeds, and pumpkin seeds.

5. Dairy Products: Milk and yogurt.

6. Fish: Salmon, tuna, and cod.

7. Meat: Beef, chicken, and turkey.

## Health Benefits of Potassium

1. Blood Pressure Management: Potassium helps lower blood pressure by counteracting the effects of sodium and promoting vasodilation, reducing the risk of hypertension and cardiovascular disease.
2. Heart Health: Supports normal heart rhythm and function, reducing the risk of arrhythmias and heart disease.
3. Stroke Prevention: Adequate potassium intake is associated with a lower risk of stroke, particularly ischemic stroke.
4. Bone Health: Some studies suggest that potassium may help maintain bone mineral density and reduce the risk of osteoporosis.
5. Muscle Function: Essential for proper muscle contraction, including the heart muscle, and helps prevent muscle weakness and cramps.
6. Kidney Health: Supports kidney function by aiding in the elimination of waste products and reducing the risk of kidney stones.
7. Electrolyte Balance: Maintains proper electrolyte balance within the body, essential for overall health and proper cellular function.

## Summary

Potassium is a crucial mineral that plays a vital role in maintaining fluid balance, muscle function, nerve transmission, heart health, and blood pressure regulation. It is found in a wide variety of foods, particularly fruits, vegetables, legumes, nuts, and seeds. Ensuring an adequate intake of potassium through a balanced diet is essential for overall health and the prevention of various chronic diseases.

4

====

# Potent Herbs and Botanicals

## Chapter 4: Potent Herbs and Botanicals

**Ashwagandha:**

Ashwagandha, also known as Withania somnifera or Indian ginseng, is a popular adaptogenic herb used in traditional Ayurvedic medicine for centuries. It is revered for its potential health benefits and is commonly used to alleviate stress, boost energy, and improve overall well- being.

## *Health Benefits of Ashwagandha*

1. Stress Reduction: Ashwagandha is known for its adaptogenic properties, meaning it helps the body adapt to stressors by regulating the release of stress hormones like cortisol. It may help reduce stress and anxiety levels and improve resilience to stress.

2. Improved Mental Health: It may help improve mood, reduce symptoms of depression and anxiety, and enhance overall mental well-being.

3. Enhanced Cognitive Function: Some research suggests that ashwagandha may improve cognitive function, memory, and concentration.
4. Boosted Energy and Stamina: Ashwagandha is believed to enhance energy levels, stamina, and endurance, making it useful for combating fatigue and improving physical performance.
5. Balanced Hormones: It may help balance hormone levels, particularly in women, and alleviate symptoms of hormonal imbalances such as irregular periods and menopausal symptoms.
6. Immune Support: Ashwagandha has immune-modulating properties that may help strengthen the immune system and enhance the body's defense against infections.
7. Anti-inflammatory Effects: It possesses anti-inflammatory properties that may help reduce inflammation and alleviate symptoms of inflammatory conditions like arthritis.
8. Heart Health: Some studies suggest that ashwagandha may help lower cholesterol levels, reduce blood pressure, and improve overall cardiovascular health.
9. Enhanced Sexual Health: Ashwagandha has been traditionally used as an aphrodisiac and may help improve sexual function and libido in both men and women.

## *Uses of Ashwagandha*

1. Stress Management: Ashwagandha supplements, such as capsules, powders, or tinctures, are commonly used to help manage stress and anxiety.
2. Energy and Vitality: It is used to boost energy levels, enhance stamina, and combat fatigue, particularly in individuals experiencing physical or mental exhaustion.

3. Mood Enhancement: Ashwagandha supplements may be used to improve mood, reduce symptoms of depression and anxiety, and promote a sense of well-being.
4. Cognitive Support: Some people use ashwagandha to enhance cognitive function, memory, and concentration, particularly during periods of intense mental activity or stress.
5. Hormonal Balance: Ashwagandha supplements are often used to support hormonal balance, alleviate symptoms of hormonal imbalances, and promote overall hormonal health.
6. Immune Boosting: It may be used to strengthen the immune system and enhance the body's ability to fight off infections, particularly during times of increased susceptibility to illness.
7. Physical Performance: Athletes and fitness enthusiasts may use ashwagandha to improve physical performance, enhance stamina, and support muscle recovery after exercise.
8. Sexual Health: It may be used to improve sexual function, libido, and overall sexual health in both men and women.

## Precautions

While ashwagandha is generally considered safe for most people when taken as recommended, it may interact with certain medications or medical conditions. Pregnant or breastfeeding women, individuals with autoimmune diseases, or those taking medications should consult a healthcare professional before using ashwagandha supplements.

Additionally, excessive intake of ashwagandha may cause digestive upset or other adverse effects in some individuals.

## Summary

Ashwagandha is a versatile herb with a wide range of potential health benefits. From stress reduction and improved mental health to enhanced physical performance and hormonal balance, ashwagandha has been used traditionally for centuries to promote overall well- being. It can be consumed in various forms, including capsules, powders, or tinctures, and is commonly used in Ayurvedic medicine to support holistic health and vitality. However, it's important to consult with a healthcare professional before using ashwagandha supplements, especially if you have any underlying health conditions or are taking medications.

**Turmeric:**

Turmeric, scientifically known as Curcuma longa, is a bright yellow-orange spice commonly used in cooking and traditional medicine. It is native to South Asia and has been used for centuries in Ayurvedic and traditional Chinese medicine for its potential health benefits.

## *Health Benefits of Turmeric*

1. Powerful Anti-Inflammatory Properties: Turmeric contains curcumin, a bioactive compound with potent anti-inflammatory effects. It may help reduce inflammation and alleviate symptoms of inflammatory conditions such as arthritis, rheumatoid arthritis, and inflammatory bowel disease.
2. Antioxidant Activity: Curcumin acts as a powerful antioxidant, helping neutralize free radicals and protect cells from oxidative damage. It may help prevent chronic diseases associated with oxidative stress, such as heart disease, cancer, and neurodegenerative disorders like Alzheimer's disease.
3. Potential Cancer Prevention: Some studies suggest that curcumin may inhibit the growth of cancer cells and prevent tumor formation. It may help reduce the risk of certain cancers, including colorectal cancer, breast cancer, and prostate cancer.
4. Heart Health: Turmeric may benefit heart health by improving endothelial function, lowering cholesterol

levels, and reducing the risk of heart disease. It may also help prevent blood clot formation and improve circulation.

5. Brain Health and Cognitive Function: Curcumin has neuroprotective properties and may help improve cognitive function, memory, and mood. It may also reduce the risk of neurodegenerative diseases like Alzheimer's and Parkinson's disease.

6. Digestive Health: Turmeric may aid digestion and promote gastrointestinal health by stimulating bile production, reducing inflammation in the gut, and protecting against digestive disorders like irritable bowel syndrome (IBS) and ulcerative colitis.

7. Pain Relief: Due to its anti-inflammatory properties, turmeric may help alleviate pain and discomfort associated with conditions like arthritis, muscle soreness, and menstrual cramps.

8. Skin Health: Turmeric has been used traditionally to treat various skin conditions, including acne, eczema, psoriasis, and wounds. It may help reduce inflammation, promote wound healing, and improve overall skin health.

## Uses of Turmeric

1. Cooking: Turmeric is commonly used as a spice in cooking, particularly in Indian cuisine. It adds flavor, color, and health benefits to dishes such as curries, soups, stews, and rice dishes.

2. Supplements: Turmeric supplements, often standardized to contain high levels of curcumin, are available in various forms, including capsules, tablets, and powders. They are used to promote overall health and well-being and may be beneficial for managing inflammatory conditions and supporting various bodily functions.

3. Tea: Turmeric tea, made by steeping turmeric powder or fresh turmeric root in hot water, is a popular beverage known for its anti-inflammatory and antioxidant properties. It may help reduce inflammation, boost immunity, and promote overall health.

4. Topical Applications: Turmeric paste or turmeric-infused oils can be applied topically to the skin to treat various skin conditions, wounds, and inflammations. It may help reduce inflammation, relieve pain, and promote wound healing.

5. Traditional Medicine: Turmeric has been used for centuries in Ayurvedic and traditional Chinese medicine to treat a wide range of health conditions, including digestive disorders, inflammatory conditions, wounds, and skin problems.

## Precautions

While turmeric is generally safe for most people when consumed in moderate amounts as a spice in food, high doses or long-term use of turmeric supplements may cause gastrointestinal upset or interact with certain medications. Pregnant or breastfeeding women, individuals with gallbladder problems, or those taking blood-thinning medications should consult a healthcare professional before using turmeric supplements.

## Summary

Turmeric is a versatile spice with numerous potential health benefits, thanks to its active compound curcumin. From reducing inflammation and oxidative stress to supporting heart health, brain function, and skin health, turmeric has been used for centuries in traditional medicine to promote overall well-being. It can be consumed as a spice in cooking, taken as a supplement, brewed into tea, or applied topically to the skin, offering various ways to incorporate its health-promoting properties into your daily routine. However, it's important to use turmeric supplements with caution and consult with a healthcare professional if you have any underlying health conditions or are taking medications.

**Ginseng:**

Ginseng is a popular herbal remedy that has been used for centuries in traditional medicine, particularly in East Asia. It is derived from the roots of plants in the Panax genus, including Panax ginseng (Asian ginseng) and Panax quinquefolius (American ginseng). Ginseng is known for its potential health benefits and is commonly used to boost energy, improve cognitive function, and enhance overall well-being.

## *Health Benefits of Ginseng*

1. Increased Energy and Stamina: Ginseng is renowned for its adaptogenic properties, which help the body adapt to stress and increase resilience. It may help improve physical endurance, reduce fatigue, and enhance overall energy levels.
2. Improved Cognitive Function: Ginseng may help improve cognitive function, memory, and concentration. It has been traditionally used to enhance mental clarity, focus, and alertness.
3. Enhanced Immune Function: Ginseng has immune-modulating properties that may help strengthen the immune system and reduce the risk of infections. It may help increase the production of immune cells and enhance immune response.
4. Stress Reduction: Ginseng may help reduce stress and anxiety levels by regulating the release of stress hormones like cortisol. It may promote a sense of calmness and relaxation.
5. Antioxidant Protection: Ginseng contains antioxidant compounds that help neutralize free radicals and protect cells from oxidative damage. It may help prevent chronic diseases associated with oxidative stress, such as heart disease, cancer, and neurodegenerative disorders.

6. Heart Health: Some studies suggest that ginseng may help improve cardiovascular health by lowering cholesterol levels, reducing inflammation, and improving blood circulation. It may help reduce the risk of heart disease and stroke.

7. Blood Sugar Regulation: Ginseng may help regulate blood sugar levels and improve insulin sensitivity, making it beneficial for individuals with diabetes or prediabetes.

8. Sexual Health: Ginseng has been traditionally used as an aphrodisiac and may help improve sexual function, libido, and fertility in both men and women. It may enhance erectile function and sexual satisfaction.

## Uses of Ginseng

1. Energy Boost: Ginseng supplements, such as capsules, tablets, or extracts, are commonly used to increase energy levels, improve stamina, and combat fatigue.

2. Cognitive Enhancement: Ginseng supplements may be used to enhance cognitive function, memory, and concentration, particularly during periods of intense mental activity or stress.

3. Immune Support: Ginseng supplements may help strengthen the immune system and reduce the risk of infections, particularly during cold and flu season or times of increased susceptibility to illness.

4. Stress Management: Ginseng supplements may be used to reduce stress and anxiety levels, promote relaxation, and improve overall well-being.

5. Heart Health: Ginseng supplements may be used to support cardiovascular health, lower cholesterol levels, reduce inflammation, and improve blood circulation.

6. Blood Sugar Regulation: Ginseng supplements may be used to help regulate blood sugar levels and improve insulin sensitivity, particularly in individuals with diabetes or prediabetes.

7. Sexual Enhancement: Ginseng supplements may be used to improve sexual function, libido, and fertility in both men and women. They may help enhance erectile function, sexual satisfaction, and overall sexual health.

## Precautions

While ginseng is generally considered safe for most people when taken as recommended, high doses or long-term use of ginseng supplements may cause side effects such as insomnia, headaches, digestive upset, and changes in blood pressure. Pregnant or breast-feeding women, individuals with certain medical conditions, or those taking medications should consult a healthcare professional before using ginseng supplements.

## Summary

Ginseng is a popular herbal remedy known for its potential health benefits, including increased energy, improved cognitive function, enhanced immune function, reduced stress, and better heart health. It is commonly used in traditional medicine to promote overall well- being and vitality. Ginseng supplements are available in various forms and may be used to support various aspects of health and wellness. However, it's important to use ginseng supplements with caution and consult with a healthcare professional if you have any underlying health conditions or are taking medications.

**Echinacea:**

Echinacea is a group of herbaceous plants in the daisy family (Asteraceae) that are native to North America. It has a long history of use in traditional Native American medicine and is commonly used today as a herbal remedy for various health purposes. The most commonly used species are Echinacea purpurea, Echinacea angustifolia, and Echinacea pallida.

## *Health Benefits of Echinacea*

1. Immune Support: Echinacea is primarily known for its immune-boosting properties. It stimulates the activity of immune cells, such as white blood cells, and enhances the body's natural defense mechanisms against infections, including viruses and bacteria.

2. Cold and Flu Prevention: Echinacea is often used to prevent and reduce the severity and duration of the common cold and flu. Some research suggests that it may help shorten the duration of cold symptoms and alleviate symptoms like cough, sore throat, and nasal congestion.

3. Respiratory Health: Echinacea may help support respiratory health and relieve symptoms of respiratory infections, such as bronchitis and sinusitis. It has mild expectorant properties and may help loosen mucus and alleviate cough.

4. Anti-inflammatory Effects: Echinacea has anti-inflammatory properties that may help reduce inflammation and alleviate symptoms of inflammatory conditions, such as arthritis and inflammatory skin conditions like eczema.

5. Antioxidant Activity: Echinacea contains antioxidant compounds that help neutralize free radicals and protect cells from oxidative damage. It may help prevent chronic diseases associated with oxidative stress, such as heart disease and cancer.

6. Wound Healing: Echinacea has been traditionally used topically to promote wound healing and alleviate symptoms of minor skin wounds, cuts, and burns. It may help reduce inflammation, prevent infection, and stimulate tissue regeneration.

7. Urinary Tract Health: Echinacea may help support urinary tract health and prevent urinary tract infections (UTIs) by enhancing immune function and reducing bacterial growth in the urinary tract.

## Uses of Echinacea

1. Cold and Flu Prevention: Echinacea supplements, such as capsules, tablets, or tinctures, are commonly used to prevent and reduce the severity and duration of the common cold and flu. They are often taken at the onset of cold symptoms or during cold and flu season.
2. Immune Support: Echinacea supplements may be used to boost immune function and enhance the body's natural defense mechanisms against infections, particularly during times of increased susceptibility to illness.
3. Respiratory Health: Echinacea supplements may be used to support respiratory health and relieve symptoms of respiratory infections, such as bronchitis, sinusitis, and the common cold. They may help alleviate cough, sore throat, and nasal congestion.
4. Anti-inflammatory Support: Echinacea supplements may be used to reduce inflammation and alleviate symptoms of inflammatory conditions, such as arthritis, inflammatory skin conditions, and autoimmune diseases.
5. Topical Applications: Echinacea extracts or ointments may be applied topically to the skin to promote wound healing and alleviate symptoms of minor skin wounds, cuts, burns, and inflammatory skin conditions.

## Precautions

While echinacea is generally considered safe for most people when taken as recommended, high doses or long-term use of echinacea supplements may cause side effects such as digestive upset, allergic reactions, and changes in blood pressure. Pregnant or breastfeeding women, individuals with certain medical conditions, or those taking medications should consult a healthcare professional before using echinacea supplements.

## *Summary*

Echinacea is a herbal remedy with a long history of use in traditional medicine for immune support, cold and flu prevention, respiratory health, wound healing, and anti-inflammatory support. It is commonly used in the form of supplements, extracts, or topical preparations to promote overall well-being and alleviate symptoms of various health conditions. However, it's important to use echinacea supplements with caution and consult with a healthcare professional if you have any underlying health conditions or are taking medications.

### **Garlic:**

Garlic, scientifically known as Allium sativum, is a popular culinary herb with a long history of use in various cultures for both culinary and medicinal purposes. It is closely related to onions, shallots, and leeks and is known for its distinctive aroma and flavor. Garlic contains several bioactive compounds, including allicin, which contribute to its potent health benefits.

## *Health Benefits of Garlic*

1. Immune Support: Garlic has immune-boosting properties and may help strengthen the immune system, reducing the risk of infections such as the common cold and flu.
2. Antibacterial and Antiviral Activity: Garlic has antimicrobial properties and may help inhibit the growth of bacteria, viruses, fungi, and parasites. It may help prevent and

alleviate symptoms of infections, including respiratory infections, gastrointestinal infections, and skin infections.

3. Heart Health: Garlic may help support heart health by lowering cholesterol levels, reducing blood pressure, and improving circulation. It may help reduce the risk of heart disease, stroke, and other cardiovascular conditions.

4. Anti-inflammatory Effects: Garlic contains compounds that have anti-inflammatory properties and may help reduce inflammation in the body. It may help alleviate symptoms of inflammatory conditions such as arthritis and inflammatory bowel disease.

5. Antioxidant Protection: Garlic is rich in antioxidants, which help neutralize free radicals and protect cells from oxidative damage. It may help prevent chronic diseases associated with oxidative stress, such as cancer, diabetes, and neurodegenerative disorders.

6. Blood Sugar Regulation: Garlic may help regulate blood sugar levels and improve insulin sensitivity, making it beneficial for individuals with diabetes or prediabetes.

7. Digestive Health: Garlic may help promote digestive health by stimulating digestion, supporting healthy gut bacteria, and reducing the risk of gastrointestinal infections.

8. Cancer Prevention: Some studies suggest that garlic may have cancer-preventive properties and may help reduce the risk of certain types of cancer, including stomach cancer, colon cancer, and prostate cancer.

## Uses of Garlic

1. Culinary Use: Garlic is commonly used as a flavoring agent in cooking, adding depth and complexity to a wide variety of dishes, including soups, sauces, stir-fries, and marinades.

2. Raw Consumption: Raw garlic cloves can be consumed on their own or added to salads, dressings, and spreads for a potent dose of health benefits.
3. Supplements: Garlic supplements, such as capsules, tablets, or extracts, are available for those who prefer a more concentrated form or for individuals who do not enjoy the taste of garlic.
4. Topical Applications: Crushed garlic cloves or garlic oil may be applied topically to the skin to treat various skin conditions, wounds, and infections. It may help reduce inflammation, prevent infection, and promote wound healing.
5. Home Remedies: Garlic has been used in various home remedies for centuries to alleviate symptoms of colds, flu, sore throat, and other respiratory infections. It may be consumed raw, infused into tea, or incorporated into homemade remedies like garlic honey or garlic oil.

## Precautions

While garlic is generally safe for most people when consumed in moderate amounts as a food or supplement, high doses or long-term use of garlic supplements may cause digestive upset,

heartburn, or allergic reactions in some individuals. Pregnant or breastfeeding women, individuals with certain medical conditions, or those taking medications should consult a healthcare professional before using garlic supplements.

## Summary

Garlic is a versatile herb with numerous potential health benefits, including immune support, heart health, anti-inflammatory effects, antioxidant protection, and cancer prevention. It is commonly used in cooking, consumed raw, taken as a supplement, or applied topically for its health-promoting properties. However, it's important to use garlic supplements with caution and consult with a healthcare professional if you have any underlying health conditions or are taking medications.

### Green Tea

Green tea, derived from the Camellia sinensis plant, is a popular beverage enjoyed worldwide for its refreshing taste and numerous health benefits. It has been consumed for centuries in traditional Chinese and Japanese medicine and is renowned for its high concentration of antioxidants and other bioactive compounds.

## *Health Benefits of Green Tea*

1. Antioxidant Properties: Green tea is rich in polyphenols, particularly catechins, which act as powerful antioxidants. These compounds help neutralize free radicals and protect cells from oxidative damage, reducing the risk of chronic diseases such as heart disease, cancer, and neurodegenerative disorders.
2. Heart Health: Regular consumption of green tea may help improve heart health by reducing levels of LDL cholesterol (the "bad" cholesterol), lowering blood pressure, and improving blood vessel function. It may help reduce the risk of heart disease and stroke.
3. Weight Management: Green tea may aid in weight loss and weight management by boosting metabolism, increasing fat oxidation, and promoting thermogenesis (the process of heat production in the body). It may help reduce body fat and abdominal fat, particularly when combined with a healthy diet and regular exercise.
4. Brain Health: Green tea contains caffeine and L-theanine, which have been shown to have beneficial effects on brain function. It may help improve cognitive function, memory, and attention, as well as enhance mood and reduce stress and anxiety.
5. Cancer Prevention: Some studies suggest that green tea may have cancer-preventive properties and may help

reduce the risk of certain types of cancer, including breast, prostate, and colorectal cancer. The antioxidant and anti-inflammatory properties of green tea may help inhibit the growth of cancer cells and reduce tumor formation.

6. Blood Sugar Regulation: Green tea may help regulate blood sugar levels and improve insulin sensitivity, making it beneficial for individuals with diabetes or prediabetes. It may help reduce the risk of type 2 diabetes and improve glycemic control.

7. Liver Health: Green tea may help support liver health by promoting liver function, reducing inflammation, and protecting against liver damage caused by toxins or oxidative stress. It may help reduce the risk of liver disease, including fatty liver disease and liver cirrhosis.

8. Skin Health: Green tea contains compounds that have anti-inflammatory and antimicrobial properties, making it beneficial for skin health. It may help reduce inflammation, fight acne-causing bacteria, and protect against UV-induced skin damage. Green tea extracts are often used in skincare products for their antioxidant and anti-aging effects.

## Uses of Green Tea

1. Beverage: Green tea is commonly consumed as a beverage, either hot or cold, and is enjoyed for its refreshing taste and potential health benefits. It can be brewed from loose tea leaves or tea bags and may be consumed plain or with added flavorings such as lemon or mint.

2. Supplements: Green tea supplements, such as capsules, tablets, or extracts, are available for those who prefer a more concentrated form or for individuals who do not enjoy the taste of green tea. They are often standardized to contain specific amounts of catechins or other bioactive compounds.

3. Cooking: Green tea leaves or matcha powder may be used in cooking and baking to add flavor and color to a variety of dishes, including soups, sauces, marinades, desserts, and baked goods.

4. Skincare: Green tea extracts or green tea-infused skincare products may be applied topically to the skin to promote skin health, reduce inflammation, fight acne, and protect against UV-induced skin damage. Green tea extracts are commonly found in moisturizers, serums, masks, and other skincare products.

## Precautions

While green tea is generally safe for most people when consumed in moderate amounts, excessive consumption of green tea or green tea supplements may cause side effects such as caffeine-related symptoms (e.g., insomnia, jitteriness, palpitations), digestive upset, or liver damage in rare cases. Pregnant or breastfeeding women, individuals with certain medical conditions (e.g., caffeine sensitivity, anxiety disorders, bleeding disorders), or those taking medications should consult a healthcare professional before consuming green tea supplements or large amounts of green tea.

## Summary

Green tea is a popular beverage enjoyed for its refreshing taste and numerous health benefits. It is rich in antioxidants and other bioactive compounds that may help reduce the risk of chronic diseases such as heart disease, cancer, and diabetes, as well as promote weight management, brain health, and skin health. Green tea can be consumed as a beverage, taken as a supplement, used in cooking, or applied topically to the skin, offering various ways to incorporate its potential health-promoting properties into your daily routine. However, it's important to use green tea supplements with caution and consult with a healthcare professional if you have any underlying health conditions or are taking medications.

5

# Specialized Supplements

## Chapter 5: Specialized Supplements

**Omega-3 Fatty Acids:**

Omega-3 fatty acids are a group of polyunsaturated fatty acids that are essential for human health and well-being. They play crucial roles in various bodily functions and have been linked to numerous health benefits.

### *Health Benefits of Omega-3 Fatty Acids*

1. Heart Health: Omega-3 fatty acids, particularly eicosapentaenoic acid (EPA) and docosahexaenoic acid (DHA), have been shown to have beneficial effects on heart health. They help reduce triglyceride levels, lower blood pressure, decrease inflammation, and improve overall cardiovascular function, reducing the risk of heart disease and stroke.

2. Brain Health: DHA, in particular, is a major component of brain cell membranes and plays a vital role in brain development and function. Omega-3 fatty acids may help improve cognitive function, memory, and mood, and may reduce the

risk of neurodegenerative diseases such as Alzheimer's disease and dementia.

3. Eye Health: DHA is also found in high concentrations in the retina of the eye and is important for maintaining optimal vision and eye health. Omega-3 fatty acids may help reduce the risk of age-related macular degeneration (AMD) and other eye conditions.

4. Inflammatory Conditions: Omega-3 fatty acids have anti-inflammatory properties and may help reduce inflammation in the body. They may be beneficial for individuals with inflammatory conditions such as rheumatoid arthritis, inflammatory bowel disease (IBD), and asthma.

5. Mood and Mental Health: Omega-3 fatty acids have been linked to improved mood and mental health. They may help reduce symptoms of depression, anxiety, and other mood disorders, and may promote overall emotional well-being.

6. Pregnancy and Infant Development: Omega-3 fatty acids are important for fetal development during pregnancy, particularly for the development of the brain and eyes. Adequate intake of omega-3 fatty acids during pregnancy and breast-feeding may help support healthy fetal growth and development.

7. Bone Health: Some studies suggest that omega-3 fatty acids may help improve bone density and reduce the risk of osteoporosis, particularly in postmenopausal women.

## Sources of Omega-3 Fatty Acids

1. Fatty Fish: Fatty fish are among the best sources of EPA and DHA omega-3 fatty acids. Examples include salmon, mackerel, sardines, trout, herring, and anchovies.

2. Fish Oil Supplements: Fish oil supplements are a convenient way to increase omega-3 fatty acid intake, particularly for individuals who do not consume enough fatty

fish in their diet. They are available in capsules or liquid form.

3. Algal Oil Supplements: Algal oil is derived from algae and is a vegetarian source of DHA omega-3 fatty acids. It is suitable for individuals following a vegetarian or vegan diet or those who prefer a plant-based alternative to fish oil.

4. Flaxseeds and Flaxseed Oil: Flaxseeds and flaxseed oil are rich in alpha-linolenic acid (ALA), a plant-based omega-3 fatty acid. However, ALA is not as readily converted to EPA and DHA in the body as EPA and DHA from fish sources.

5. Chia Seeds: Chia seeds are another plant-based source of ALA omega-3 fatty acids. They can be added to smoothies, yogurt, oatmeal, or baked goods for a nutritional boost.

6. Walnuts: Walnuts are one of the few nuts that contain significant amounts of ALA omega- 3 fatty acids. They can be eaten as a snack or added to salads, cereals, or baked goods.

7. Hemp Seeds: Hemp seeds are rich in ALA omega-3 fatty acids and can be sprinkled on salads, yogurt, or cereal, or incorporated into smoothies or energy bars.

## *Summary*

Omega-3 fatty acids are essential nutrients that play important roles in heart health, brain function, eye health, inflammation, mood regulation, and overall well-being. They are found in fatty fish, fish oil supplements, algal oil supplements, flaxseeds, flaxseed oil, chia seeds, walnuts, and hemp seeds. Incorporating omega-3-rich foods into your diet or taking omega-3 supplements can help support optimal health and reduce the risk of chronic diseases.

### Probiotics:

Probiotics are live microorganisms that confer health benefits when consumed in adequate amounts. They are commonly referred to as "good" or "friendly" bacteria and are believed to promote a healthy balance of gut bacteria, also known as the gut microbiota or gut flora.

Probiotics can be found in certain foods, supplements, and fermented products.

## Health Benefits of Probiotics

1. Digestive Health: Probiotics help maintain a healthy balance of beneficial bacteria in the gut, which is essential for optimal digestive function. They may help alleviate symptoms of digestive disorders such as irritable bowel syndrome (IBS), inflammatory bowel disease (IBD), diarrhea, constipation, and gastroenteritis.
2. Immune Support: Probiotics play a role in supporting immune function by enhancing the body's natural defense mechanisms. They help regulate immune responses and may help reduce the risk of infections, allergies, and autoimmune diseases.
3. Mood and Mental Health: There is growing evidence suggesting a link between gut health and mental health, known as the gut-brain axis. Probiotics may help improve mood, reduce symptoms of depression and anxiety, and promote overall mental well-being by influencing neurotransmitter production and communication between the gut and the brain.
4. Women's Health: Probiotics may help support women's health by promoting vaginal health and preventing vaginal infections such as bacterial vaginosis and yeast infections. They may also help reduce the risk of urinary tract infections (UTIs).
5. Skin Health: Some research suggests that probiotics may benefit skin health by reducing inflammation, promoting wound healing, and alleviating symptoms of skin conditions such as acne, eczema, and psoriasis.
6. Weight Management: Probiotics may play a role in weight management by influencing the balance of gut bacteria involved in energy metabolism, appetite regulation, and fat storage. They

may help reduce body fat, improve insulin sensitivity, and support healthy weight loss.

7. Heart Health: Certain strains of probiotics may help support heart health by lowering cholesterol levels, reducing blood pressure, and improving markers of cardiovascular risk.

## *Sources of Probiotics*

1. Fermented Foods: Fermented foods are natural sources of probiotics and include yogurt, kefir, sauerkraut, kimchi, tempeh, miso, kombucha, and pickles. These foods undergo fermentation by beneficial bacteria, which increases their probiotic content.

2. Probiotic Supplements: Probiotic supplements are available in various forms, including capsules, tablets, powders, and liquids. They contain specific strains of beneficial bacteria in controlled amounts and are often used to target specific health conditions or to replenish gut flora after antibiotic use.

3. Dairy Products: Some dairy products, such as yogurt and kefir, contain added probiotic strains, such as Lactobacillus and Bifidobacterium. These products may provide additional probiotic benefits beyond their natural bacterial content.

4. Non-Dairy Products: Probiotic-containing non-dairy products, such as soy yogurt, coconut yogurt, and non-dairy kefir, are available for individuals who are lactose intolerant or following a vegan or dairy-free diet.

5. Supplemented Foods: Some foods, such as certain cereals, granola bars, juices, and snacks, are fortified with probiotics to enhance their nutritional value and health benefits.

## *Summary*

Probiotics are beneficial microorganisms that play a key role in maintaining digestive health, supporting immune function, promoting mental well-being, and benefiting overall health.

They can be found in fermented foods, probiotic supplements, dairy products, non-dairy products, and supplemented foods. Incorporating probiotic-rich foods into your diet or taking probiotic supplements can help maintain a healthy balance of gut bacteria and support optimal health and well-being.

**Glucosamine:**

Glucosamine is a naturally occurring compound found in the body, particularly in the fluid that surrounds joints. It is commonly used as a dietary supplement to support joint health, especially in individuals with osteoarthritis or other joint-related conditions. Glucosamine is often combined with chondroitin sulfate, another compound found in cartilage, in joint health supplements.

## *Health Benefits of Glucosamine*

1. Joint Health: Glucosamine is a building block for cartilage, the flexible tissue that cushions joints and helps maintain joint mobility and flexibility. Supplementation with glucosamine may help support joint health, reduce joint pain and stiffness, and improve overall joint function, particularly in individuals with osteoarthritis or other degenerative joint conditions.

2. Cartilage Repair: Glucosamine may help stimulate the production of proteoglycans and collagen, which are essential components of cartilage. It may help promote cartilage repair and regeneration, potentially slowing down the progression of osteoarthritis and preserving joint function.

3. Inflammation Reduction: Some research suggests that glucosamine may have anti- inflammatory effects, helping

reduce inflammation in the joints and alleviate symptoms of inflammatory joint conditions such as osteoarthritis and rheumatoid arthritis.

4. Pain Relief: Glucosamine supplementation may help reduce joint pain and discomfort, improve mobility, and enhance overall quality of life in individuals with osteoarthritis or other joint-related conditions. It may be particularly beneficial for individuals who are unable to tolerate nonsteroidal anti-inflammatory drugs (NSAIDs) or other pain medications.

5. Bone Health: Glucosamine may also have benefits for bone health, as it is involved in the production of glycosaminoglycans, which are important components of bone tissue. It may help support bone density and strength, reducing the risk of osteoporosis and fractures.

## Sources of Glucosamine

1. Shellfish: Glucosamine is naturally found in the shells of shellfish such as crab, shrimp, lobster, and crayfish. Shellfish-derived glucosamine supplements are a common source of glucosamine for individuals who are unable to obtain sufficient amounts from dietary sources.

2. Vegetarian Sources: Glucosamine supplements are also available in vegetarian forms derived from fungal sources such as Aspergillus niger or from plant-based sources such as corn. These vegetarian glucosamine supplements are suitable for individuals who prefer non-animal-derived sources.

3. Joint Health Supplements: Glucosamine is commonly found in joint health supplements, often in combination with chondroitin sulfate, MSM (methylsulfonylmethane), or other ingredients designed to support joint health and reduce joint pain and inflammation.

## Summary

Glucosamine is a naturally occurring compound found in the body, particularly in the fluid that surrounds joints. It plays a crucial role in supporting joint health, cartilage repair, inflammation reduction, pain relief, and bone health. Glucosamine supplements are commonly used to support joint health and alleviate symptoms of osteoarthritis and other joint-related conditions. Glucosamine can be obtained from dietary sources such as shellfish or vegetarian sources, as well as through supplementation. If you're considering glucosamine supplementation, it's advisable to consult with a healthcare professional, especially if you have any existing health conditions or are taking medications.

**Melatonin:**

Melatonin is a hormone produced naturally by the pineal gland in the brain in response to darkness. It plays a crucial role in regulating the sleep-wake cycle and is often referred to as the "sleep hormone." Melatonin supplements are commonly used to promote sleep and manage sleep-related disorders, as well as for other potential health benefits.

## Health Benefits of Melatonin

1. Sleep Regulation: Melatonin is best known for its role in regulating the sleep-wake cycle. It helps synchronize the body's internal clock with the natural light-dark cycle, promoting sleepiness at night and wakefulness during the day. Melatonin supplements are commonly used to improve sleep quality, reduce the time it takes to fall asleep (sleep latency), and manage sleep disorders such as insomnia, jet lag, and shift work sleep disorder.

2. Jet Lag and Travel: Melatonin supplements may help alleviate symptoms of jet lag, such as fatigue, daytime sleepiness,

and difficulty sleeping, by adjusting the body's internal clock to a new time zone. Taking melatonin supplements at the appropriate time before
bedtime may help speed up the adjustment process and reduce the severity of jet lag symptoms.

3. Shift Work Sleep Disorder: Melatonin supplements may be beneficial for individuals who work non-traditional hours or rotating shifts and experience disruptions to their sleep- wake cycle. Taking melatonin supplements at specific times may help improve sleep quality, reduce sleep disturbances, and promote better daytime functioning in shift workers.

4. Sleep Disorders: Melatonin supplements may be helpful for individuals with certain sleep disorders, such as delayed sleep phase disorder (DSPD), non-24-hour sleep-wake disorder (Non-24), and rapid eye movement sleep behavior disorder (RBD). Melatonin supplementation may help regulate the sleep-wake cycle and improve sleep quality in individuals with these conditions.

5. Antioxidant Protection: Melatonin is a potent antioxidant that helps neutralize free radicals and protect cells from oxidative damage. It may help reduce oxidative stress, inflammation, and cell damage, and may have potential benefits for various health conditions associated with oxidative stress, such as heart disease, neurodegenerative disorders, and aging.

6. Immune Function: Some research suggests that melatonin may have immune-modulating effects and may help regulate immune function. It may help enhance immune responses, reduce inflammation, and improve overall immune health, particularly in individuals with compromised immune systems or chronic inflammatory conditions.

## *Sources of Melatonin*

1. Dietary Sources: Melatonin is naturally found in certain foods, particularly fruits such as tart cherries, grapes, and bananas, as well as nuts such as almonds and walnuts. Consuming these foods may provide small amounts of melatonin, although it is unlikely to be sufficient for therapeutic purposes.

2. Supplements: Melatonin supplements are available in various forms, including tablets, capsules, sublingual tablets, liquid drops, and extended-release formulations. They are commonly used to promote sleep and manage sleep-related disorders. Melatonin supplements are typically taken orally, preferably 30 minutes to an hour before bedtime, to facilitate the onset of sleep.

## *Summary*

Melatonin is a hormone produced naturally by the pineal gland in the brain in response to darkness. It plays a crucial role in regulating the sleep-wake cycle and is commonly used as a

supplement to promote sleep and manage sleep-related disorders. Melatonin supplements may also have antioxidant, immune-modulating, and potential health benefits beyond sleep regulation. While melatonin supplements are generally considered safe for short-term use, it's advisable to consult with a healthcare professional before using them, especially if you have any underlying health conditions or are taking medications.

**L-Theanine:**

L-Theanine is an amino acid found naturally in tea leaves, particularly in green tea (Camellia sinensis). It is known for its calming and relaxing effects and is commonly used as a dietary supplement to promote relaxation, reduce stress, and improve cognitive function. L-Theanine is believed to work synergistically with caffeine, another compound found in tea, to promote a state of alertness and focus without causing the jittery feelings often associated with caffeine consumption.

## *Health Benefits of L-Theanine*

1. Stress Reduction: L-Theanine has been shown to have calming and relaxing effects on the brain, helping reduce feelings of stress and anxiety. It may help promote relaxation without causing drowsiness, making it beneficial for individuals dealing with everyday stressors or anxiety-related disorders.

2. Improved Sleep Quality: L-Theanine may help improve sleep quality and duration by promoting relaxation and reducing stress levels. It may help individuals fall asleep faster, stay asleep longer, and experience deeper, more restorative sleep.

3. Enhanced Cognitive Function: L-Theanine has been studied for its potential cognitive- enhancing effects. It may help improve attention, focus, and concentration, as well as memory and learning ability. L-Theanine is believed to work synergistically with caffeine to promote a state of alertness and mental clarity, without the jittery side effects often associated with caffeine consumption.

4. Mood Regulation: L-Theanine may help regulate mood and promote a sense of well-being. It may help balance neurotransmitter levels in the brain, such as serotonin, dopamine, and gamma-aminobutyric acid (GABA), which play important roles in mood regulation and emotional stability.

5. Blood Pressure Regulation: Some research suggests that L-Theanine may help regulate blood pressure levels, particularly in individuals with hypertension (high blood pressure).
It may help reduce blood pressure by promoting relaxation and reducing stress, although more research is needed to confirm its effectiveness for this purpose.

6. Antioxidant Protection: L-Theanine is a potent antioxidant that helps neutralize free radicals and protect cells from oxidative damage. It may help reduce inflammation, support immune function, and promote overall health and well-being.

## Sources of L-Theanine

1. Tea: L-Theanine is naturally found in tea leaves, particularly in green tea (Camellia sinensis). Green tea contains relatively high levels of L-Theanine compared to other types of tea, such as black tea or oolong tea. Drinking green tea is a natural way to consume L- Theanine and may provide relaxation and other health benefits associated with this amino acid.

2. Supplements: L-Theanine supplements are available in various forms, including capsules, tablets, and powder. They are commonly used to promote relaxation, reduce stress, improve sleep quality, and enhance cognitive function. L-Theanine supplements are often taken orally and may be used on their own or in combination with other nutrients or herbs for synergistic effects.

## *Summary*

L-Theanine is an amino acid found naturally in tea leaves, particularly in green tea. It is known for its calming and relaxing effects and is commonly used as a dietary supplement to promote relaxation, reduce stress, improve sleep quality, and enhance cognitive function. L-Theanine is believed to work synergistically with caffeine to promote alertness and mental clarity without causing jittery feelings. Consuming green tea or taking L-Theanine supplements may provide relaxation and other health benefits associated with this amino acid.

# Supplements for Specific Health Conditions

## Chapter 6: Supplements for Specific Health Conditions

**Supplements for Immune Support:**

Vitamin C: Vitamin C is a powerful antioxidant that supports immune function by stimulating the production of white blood cells, which help

protect the body against infections. It also helps boost collagen production and supports skin health. Foods rich in vitamin C include citrus fruits, strawberries, kiwi, bell peppers, and broccoli.

1. Vitamin D: Vitamin D plays a crucial role in immune regulation and helps enhance the function of immune cells. Adequate vitamin D levels may help reduce the risk of respiratory infections and other immune-related conditions. Natural sources of vitamin D include sunlight exposure, fatty fish, egg yolks, and fortified foods.
2. Zinc: Zinc is an essential mineral that plays a key role in immune function and wound healing. It helps support

the activity of various immune cells and is involved in the production of antibodies. Zinc supplementation may help reduce the duration and severity of colds and other infections. Food sources of zinc include oysters, beef, chicken, nuts, seeds, and legumes.

3. Probiotics: Probiotics are beneficial bacteria that help maintain a healthy balance of gut bacteria, which is essential for optimal immune function. Probiotic supplements may help support immune health by enhancing the gut microbiota and promoting immune responses. Probiotic-rich foods include yogurt, kefir, sauerkraut, kimchi, and kombucha.

4. Echinacea: Echinacea is an herbal supplement commonly used to support immune function and reduce the severity and duration of colds and flu. It may help stimulate the activity of immune cells and enhance the body's natural defense mechanisms against infections.

5. Elderberry: Elderberry is a traditional herbal remedy known for its immune-boosting properties. Elderberry supplements, particularly elderberry syrup or extract, may help reduce the severity and duration of colds and flu by supporting immune function and reducing inflammation.

6. Garlic: Garlic contains compounds with immune-boosting and antimicrobial properties that may help support immune function and reduce the risk of infections. Garlic supplements or raw garlic cloves may help enhance the body's natural defense mechanisms against pathogens.

7. Selenium: Selenium is a trace mineral that plays a critical role in immune function and antioxidant defense. It helps support the activity of immune cells and protects cells from oxidative damage. Selenium supplementation may help enhance immune responses and reduce the risk of infections. Good food sources of selenium include Brazil nuts, fish, poultry, eggs, and whole grains.

**Supplements for Bone Health:** Calcium: Calcium is a mineral that is essential for building and maintaining strong bones and teeth. Adequate calcium intake is important throughout life, particularly during childhood, adolescence, and older adulthood when bone density may decline. Good food sources of calcium include dairy products, leafy green vegetables (such as kale and broccoli), fortified foods (such as fortified plant-based milk and orange juice), and fish with edible bones (such as canned salmon and sardines). Calcium supplements are available in various forms, including calcium carbonate and calcium citrate, and may be beneficial for individuals who do not consume enough calcium through diet alone.

1. Vitamin D: Vitamin D is necessary for calcium absorption and plays a crucial role in bone health. It helps regulate calcium and phosphorus levels in the blood and supports bone mineralization. Vitamin D is synthesized in the skin in response to sunlight exposure and can also be obtained from dietary sources such as fatty fish (such as salmon and mackerel), egg yolks, fortified foods (such as fortified milk and cereal), and supplements. Vitamin D supplements, particularly vitamin D3, may be recommended for individuals with inadequate sun exposure or low dietary intake of vitamin D.

2. Vitamin K: Vitamin K is important for bone metabolism and helps regulate calcium deposition in bones. It plays a role in synthesizing proteins involved in bone mineralization and may help improve bone density and reduce the risk of fractures. Good food sources of vitamin K include leafy green vegetables (such as spinach, kale, and Swiss chard), broccoli, Brussels sprouts, and fermented foods (such as natto and sauerkraut). Vitamin K supplements, particularly vitamin K2, may be beneficial for individuals with low dietary intake of vitamin K or impaired vitamin K absorption.

3. Magnesium: Magnesium is involved in bone formation and helps regulate calcium metabolism. It plays a role in activating

vitamin D and stimulating the production of calcitonin, a hormone that helps regulate calcium levels in the blood. Good food sources of magnesium include nuts, seeds, whole grains, leafy green vegetables, legumes, and fortified foods. Magnesium supplements may be beneficial for individuals with low dietary intake of magnesium or impaired magnesium absorption.

4. Phosphorus: Phosphorus is a mineral that is important for bone health and helps form the structure of bones and teeth. It works together with calcium to maintain bone density and strength. Good food sources of phosphorus

include dairy products, meat, fish, poultry, nuts, seeds, and whole grains. Phosphorus supplements are generally not necessary for individuals with a balanced diet, as most people consume an adequate amount of phosphorus through food alone.

5. Boron: Boron is a trace mineral that may help support bone health by improving calcium absorption and utilization, stimulating the production of estrogen and testosterone, and reducing inflammation. Good food sources of boron include fruits (such as apples, pears, and grapes), vegetables (such as broccoli, carrots, and potatoes), nuts, legumes, and avocado. Boron supplements may be beneficial for individuals with low dietary intake of boron or impaired boron absorption.

**Supplements for Heart Health:** Omega-3 Fatty Acids: Omega-3 fatty acids, particularly eicosapentaenoic acid (EPA) and docosahexaenoic acid (DHA), are essential fats that play a crucial role in heart health. They help reduce triglyceride levels, lower blood pressure, decrease inflammation, and improve overall cardiovascular function. Omega-3 supplements are available in the form of fish oil capsules, krill oil capsules, and algal oil capsules (for vegetarians and vegans).

1. Coenzyme Q10 (CoQ10): Coenzyme Q10 is a compound that is naturally produced by the body and is involved in energy

production in cells. It also acts as a potent antioxidant, protecting cells from oxidative damage. CoQ10 supplements may help support heart health by improving energy metabolism in the heart muscle, reducing inflammation, and promoting antioxidant protection.

2. Magnesium: Magnesium is an essential mineral that plays a critical role in heart function and cardiovascular health. It helps regulate blood pressure, maintain normal heart rhythm, and support muscle function. Magnesium supplements may help reduce the risk of cardiovascular disease and improve overall heart health, particularly in individuals with low dietary intake of magnesium or magnesium deficiency.

3. Garlic: Garlic contains compounds with heart-protective properties, including allicin, which may help reduce cholesterol levels, lower blood pressure, and improve circulation. Garlic supplements may help support heart health by reducing the risk of cardiovascular disease and improving cardiovascular function.

4. Fiber: Soluble fiber, such as psyllium husk, oat bran, and glucomannan, can help lower cholesterol levels and improve heart health by reducing the absorption of cholesterol from the digestive tract and promoting the excretion of bile acids. Fiber supplements may help support heart health when consumed as part of a healthy diet rich in fruits, vegetables, whole grains, and legumes.

5. Plant Sterols and Stanols: Plant sterols and stanols are compounds found naturally in fruits, vegetables, nuts, seeds, and vegetable oils. They help lower LDL (bad) cholesterol levels by blocking the absorption of cholesterol from the digestive tract. Plant sterol and stanol supplements may help reduce the risk of heart disease when consumed as part of a heart-healthy diet.

6. Hawthorn: Hawthorn is an herbal supplement that has been traditionally used to support heart health and improve cardiovascular function. It may help dilate blood vessels,

improve blood flow, lower blood pressure, and reduce the risk of heart failure. Hawthorn supplements may be beneficial for individuals with mild to moderate heart conditions.

7. L-Arginine: L-arginine is an amino acid that plays a role in nitric oxide production, which helps dilate blood vessels and improve blood flow. L-arginine supplements may help lower blood pressure, improve circulation, and support cardiovascular health, particularly in individuals with hypertension or endothelial dysfunction.

**Supplements for Mental Wellness:** Omega-3 Fatty Acids: Omega-3 fatty acids, particularly eicosapentaenoic acid (EPA) and docosahexaenoic acid (DHA), are essential fats that play a crucial role in brain health and cognitive function. They help support neuronal structure and function, reduce inflammation in the brain, and promote the production of neurotransmitters associated with mood regulation. Omega-3 supplements, such as fish oil or algal oil capsules, may help improve mood, reduce symptoms of depression and anxiety, and support overall mental wellness.

1. Vitamin D: Vitamin D is important for brain health and cognitive function, as well as for mood regulation. Adequate vitamin D levels have been associated with a reduced risk of depression, anxiety, and other mood disorders. Vitamin D supplements may be beneficial, particularly for individuals with low sunlight exposure or vitamin D deficiency.

2. B-Vitamins: B-vitamins, including vitamin B6, vitamin B12, and folate (vitamin B9), play a key role in neurotransmitter synthesis and function. They help support the production of serotonin, dopamine, and other neurotransmitters involved in mood regulation. B-vitamin supplements or B-complex supplements may help improve mood, reduce stress, and support cognitive function.

3. Magnesium: Magnesium is an essential mineral that plays a role in neurotransmitter regulation, stress response, and mood modulation. It helps support the production of serotonin and may help reduce symptoms of anxiety and depression. Magnesium supplements may be beneficial for individuals with low dietary intake of magnesium or magnesium deficiency.

4. L-Theanine: L-Theanine is an amino acid found naturally in tea leaves, particularly in green tea. It has calming and relaxing effects and may help reduce stress, anxiety, and promote relaxation without causing drowsiness. L-Theanine supplements may help support mental wellness and improve cognitive function.

5. Rhodiola Rosea: Rhodiola Rosea is an adaptogenic herb that has been traditionally used to reduce stress, improve mood, and enhance mental performance. It may help increase resistance to stress, reduce fatigue, and improve overall mental well-being. Rhodiola supplements may be beneficial for individuals experiencing chronic stress or mental fatigue.

6. Ashwagandha: Ashwagandha is an adaptogenic herb that has been used in traditional Ayurvedic medicine for centuries to reduce stress, anxiety, and promote relaxation. It may help improve mood, reduce cortisol levels, and support adrenal function. Ashwagandha supplements may be beneficial for individuals experiencing stress-related symptoms or mood disturbances.

7. Ginkgo Biloba: Ginkgo Biloba is an herbal supplement that has been used to support cognitive function and memory. It may help improve blood flow to the brain, enhance cognitive performance, and support overall mental wellness. Ginkgo Biloba supplements may be beneficial for individuals looking to maintain cognitive function and memory as they age.

**Supplements for Digestive Health:** Probiotics: Probiotics are beneficial bacteria that help maintain a healthy balance of gut microbiota, which is essential for proper digestion and immune function. Probiotic supplements contain live bacteria strains that can help populate the gut with beneficial microbes, improve digestion, and support overall gut health.

Look for probiotic supplements containing various strains of Lactobacillus and Bifidobacterium, which are commonly found in the gut.

1. Digestive Enzymes: Digestive enzymes help break down carbohydrates, proteins, and fats into smaller molecules that can be absorbed and utilized by the body. Supplementing with digestive enzyme supplements may help improve digestion, reduce bloating, gas, and indigestion, and support nutrient absorption. Look for enzyme supplements containing a blend of enzymes such as amylase, protease, lipase, cellulase, and lactase.

2. Fiber: Fiber is essential for maintaining regular bowel movements, promoting healthy digestion, and supporting gut health. Soluble fiber, such as psyllium husk, flaxseed, and acacia fiber, helps soften stools and promote bowel regularity, while insoluble fiber, such as wheat bran and cellulose, adds bulk to stools and helps prevent constipation. Fiber supplements may be beneficial for individuals who do not consume enough fiber through diet alone.

3. L-Glutamine: L-Glutamine is an amino acid that plays a crucial role in maintaining the integrity of the intestinal lining and supporting gut health. It helps repair damaged intestinal mucosa, reduce inflammation, and support immune function in the gut. L-Glutamine supplements may be beneficial for individuals with leaky gut syndrome,
irritable bowel syndrome (IBS), or other gastrointestinal conditions.

4. Aloe Vera: Aloe vera is a plant known for its soothing and healing properties, particularly for the digestive tract. Aloe

vera supplements or aloe vera juice may help soothe gastro-intestinal inflammation, reduce symptoms of heartburn, acid reflux, and irritable bowel syndrome (IBS), and promote over-all digestive health.

5. Peppermint Oil: Peppermint oil is an herbal remedy that has been traditionally used to relieve digestive symptoms such as bloating, gas, and indigestion. It helps relax the muscles of the digestive tract, reduce spasms, and improve digestion. Peppermint oil supplements may be beneficial for individuals with irritable bowel syndrome (IBS) or functional dyspepsia.

6. Ginger: Ginger is a spice with anti-inflammatory and digestive properties that may help soothe gastrointestinal discomfort, reduce nausea, and improve digestion. Ginger supplements or ginger tea may be beneficial for individuals experiencing digestive symptoms such as indigestion, bloating, or nausea.

7. Turmeric: Turmeric contains curcumin, a compound with anti-inflammatory and antioxidant properties that may help reduce inflammation in the digestive tract, support gut health, and relieve symptoms of digestive disorders such as inflammatory bowel disease (IBD) and irritable bowel syndrome (IBS). Turmeric supplements or turmeric tea may be beneficial for individuals looking to support digestive health.

**Supplements for Skin and Hair Health:** Collagen: Collagen is a protein that provides structure and elasticity to the skin and helps maintain healthy hair and nails. Collagen supplements may help support skin elasticity, reduce the appearance of wrinkles and fine lines, and promote hair growth and strength. Collagen peptides supplements, derived from collagen protein broken down into smaller peptides for better absorption, are commonly used for skin and hair health.

1. Vitamin C: Vitamin C is a powerful antioxidant that plays a crucial role in collagen synthesis, skin repair, and protection

against oxidative damage. It helps promote a youthful complexion, reduce hyperpigmentation and sun damage, and support overall skin health. Vitamin C supplements may help support skin health when consumed orally or applied topically in skincare products.

2. Vitamin E: Vitamin E is a fat-soluble antioxidant that helps protect skin cells from oxidative damage caused by free radicals and UV radiation. It helps promote skin healing, reduce inflammation, and support overall skin health.
Vitamin E supplements or vitamin E oil applied topically may help improve skin texture, hydration, and appearance.

3. Biotin: Biotin, also known as vitamin B7 or vitamin H, is a water-soluble vitamin that plays a key role in promoting healthy hair, skin, and nails. It helps support keratin production, a protein that makes up the structure of hair and nails. Biotin supplements may help improve hair growth, thickness, and strength, as well as promote nail health and reduce brittleness.

4. Omega-3 Fatty Acids: Omega-3 fatty acids, particularly EPA and DHA, are essential fats that play a crucial role in skin health and hydration. They help maintain the integrity of the skin barrier, reduce inflammation, and support overall skin health. Omega-3 supplements, such as fish oil or algal oil capsules, may help improve skin hydration, texture, and appearance.

5. Zinc: Zinc is a trace mineral that plays a role in skin health, wound healing, and immune function. It helps regulate oil production, reduce inflammation, and support collagen synthesis. Zinc supplements may help improve acne symptoms, promote wound healing, and support overall skin health.

6. Silica: Silica is a mineral that is important for maintaining healthy skin, hair, and nails. It helps support collagen production, improve skin elasticity, and strengthen hair and nails. Silica supplements derived from bamboo extract or horsetail extract may help support skin and hair health.

7. Astaxanthin: Astaxanthin is a powerful antioxidant found in certain microalgae and seafood. It helps protect skin cells from oxidative damage caused by UV radiation and environmental pollutants, reduce inflammation, and promote skin hydration and elasticity. Astaxanthin supplements may help support skin health and reduce signs of aging.

## CONCLUSION: RECAP OF KEY POINTS

1. Supplements are Not a Substitute for a Healthy Diet: While supplements can be beneficial, they should not replace a balanced diet rich in fruits, vegetables, whole grains, lean proteins, and healthy fats. Food provides a wide array of nutrients and compounds that work synergistically to support overall health and well-being.

2. Consult with a Healthcare Professional: It's important to consult with a healthcare professional before starting any new supplements, especially if you have any underlying health conditions, are pregnant or breastfeeding, or are taking medications. A healthcare professional can help determine if supplements are appropriate for you and recommend the right dosage and formulation.

3. Quality Matters: Choose high-quality supplements from reputable brands that undergo third-party testing for purity, potency, and safety. Look for supplements that are certified
by independent organizations such as USP, NSF, or ConsumerLab.com to ensure quality and reliability.

4. Start Slowly and Monitor Effects: When starting a new supplement regimen, start with a low dose and gradually increase as needed. Pay attention to how your body responds and monitor for any adverse effects or interactions with medications.

5. Consider Individual Needs: Everyone's nutritional needs are different, and supplements should be

tailored to individual needs and deficiencies. Consider factors such as age, gender, health status, lifestyle, and dietary preferences when choosing supplements.

6. Focus on Nutrient Gaps: Supplements can help fill nutrient gaps in the diet, especially for nutrients that may be lacking or difficult to obtain enough of through food alone. Focus on supplements that address specific deficiencies or support particular health goals.

7. Use as Directed: Follow the recommended dosage and instructions for use provided on the supplement label or as directed by a healthcare professional. Avoid exceeding the recommended dosage unless advised by a healthcare professional, as excessive intake of certain nutrients can have adverse effects.

8. Be Wary of Claims: Be skeptical of exaggerated claims or promises made by supplement manufacturers. While supplements can support overall health and well-being, they are not miracle cures and cannot replace healthy lifestyle habits such as regular exercise, stress management, and adequate sleep.

By keeping these key points in mind, you can make informed decisions about incorporating supplements into your wellness routine and maximize their potential benefits while minimizing risks.

Balanced nutrition forms the foundation of overall health and well-being, providing the body with essential nutrients it needs to function optimally. Here are the key reasons why balanced nutrition is important, along with the role that supplements can play:

1. Meeting Nutritional Needs: A balanced diet provides the body with the right balance of macronutrients (carbohydrates, proteins, and fats) and micronutrients (vitamins and minerals) needed for growth, development, energy production,

and immune function. Each nutrient plays a specific role in the body, and deficiencies can lead to a range of health problems.

2. Supporting Overall Health: Balanced nutrition supports overall health and reduces the risk of chronic diseases such as heart disease, diabetes, obesity, and certain cancers. Consuming a variety of nutrient-rich foods promotes optimal health and well-being, while poor dietary habits can increase the risk of nutrient deficiencies and health problems.

3. Promoting Optimal Growth and Development: Proper nutrition is essential for children's growth and development, providing the nutrients needed for healthy bones, muscles, organs, and cognitive function. A balanced diet supports physical growth, cognitive development, and immune function in children and adolescents.

4. Maintaining a Healthy Weight: A balanced diet helps maintain a healthy weight by providing the body with the right balance of calories and nutrients. Consuming a variety of nutrient-dense foods, such as fruits, vegetables, whole grains, lean proteins, and healthy fats, helps control hunger, regulate appetite, and support weight management.

5. Boosting Energy Levels: Balanced nutrition provides the energy needed for physical activity, mental alertness, and daily activities. Carbohydrates are the body's primary source of energy, while proteins and fats provide sustained energy and support metabolism. Consuming a balanced diet helps maintain stable blood sugar levels and prevents energy crashes.

6. Supporting Immune Function: Proper nutrition is essential for a healthy immune system, providing the vitamins, minerals, and antioxidants needed to support immune function and defend against infections. Nutrient-rich foods, such as fruits, vegetables, whole grains, and lean proteins, contain immune-boosting nutrients that help strengthen the body's defenses.

While balanced nutrition is crucial for overall health, supplements can complement a healthy diet by filling nutrient gaps, addressing specific deficiencies, and supporting particular health goals. Here's how supplements can be beneficial:

1. Filling Nutrient Gaps: Supplements can help fill nutrient gaps in the diet, especially for nutrients that may be lacking or difficult to obtain enough of through food alone. For example, vitamin D, omega-3 fatty acids, and certain minerals may be obtained from supplements to ensure adequate intake.

2. Supporting Specific Health Goals: Supplements can support specific health goals or address individual needs, such as promoting bone health, supporting heart health, improving skin and hair health, or boosting immune function. Supplements containing targeted nutrients or herbal extracts may be used to support particular health goals or address specific health concerns.

3. Compensating for Dietary Restrictions: Supplements can be beneficial for individuals with dietary restrictions, such as vegetarians, vegans, or individuals with food allergies or intolerances. Certain nutrients may be obtained from supplements to compensate for dietary restrictions and ensure adequate intake.

4. Enhancing Performance: Some supplements may be used to enhance athletic performance, support recovery, or improve endurance and stamina. Athletes and active individuals may use supplements such as protein powders, creatine, or branched-chain amino acids to support muscle growth, recovery, and performance.

While supplements can be beneficial when used appropriately, they are not a substitute for a healthy diet, and they should not replace nutrient-rich foods. It's important to prioritize a balanced diet and lifestyle habits that support overall health and well-being. Additionally, it's advisable to consult with a healthcare professional before starting any new supplements, especially if you have any underlying health conditions or are taking medications.

# Consultation with Healthcare Professionals

1. **Importance of Consultation:** Healthcare professionals, such as doctors, registered dietitians, pharmacists, or certified nutritionists, can provide personalized guidance and recommendations regarding supplement use based on your individual health status, medical history, and specific needs. Consulting with a healthcare professional can help you make informed decisions about which supplements to take, how to take them, and what dosage is appropriate for you.

2. Health Assessment: During a consultation, a healthcare professional will conduct a health assessment to gather information about your medical history, current health status, dietary habits, lifestyle factors, and any medications or supplements you are currently taking. This information helps the healthcare professional understand your unique health needs and identify any potential interactions or contraindications with supplements.

3. Discussion of Goals and Concerns: You will have the opportunity to discuss your health goals, concerns, and reasons for considering supplement use with the healthcare professional. Whether you're looking to address specific health issues, support athletic performance, or optimize overall wellness, the healthcare professional can provide tailored recommendations to help you achieve your goals safely and effectively.

4. Evaluation of Nutrient Status: If necessary, the healthcare professional may recommend laboratory tests or assessments to evaluate your nutrient status and identify any nutrient deficiencies or imbalances that may warrant supplementation. These tests can

   help determine which supplements are appropriate for you and ensure that you are taking the right nutrients in the right amounts.

5. Guidance on Supplement Selection: Based on your health assessment and goals, the healthcare professional can recommend specific supplements that are suitable for your needs. They can provide information about the benefits, risks, and potential side effects of various supplements, as well as guidance on selecting high-quality products from reputable brands.

6. **Dosage and Administration:** The healthcare professional can provide guidance on the appropriate dosage, timing, and administration of supplements based on your individual health needs and preferences. They can advise you on how to take supplements safely and effectively to maximize their benefits while minimizing the risk of adverse effects or interactions with medications.

7. Monitoring and Follow-Up: After starting a supplement regimen, it's important to monitor your response and any changes in your health status. The healthcare professional can provide ongoing support, monitoring, and follow-up to ensure that

the supplements are meeting your needs and are being used safely and effectively. They can also make adjustments to your supplement regimen as needed based on your progress and any changes in your health status.

Overall, consulting with a healthcare professional about supplements can help you make informed decisions, optimize your supplement regimen, and ensure that you are taking supplements safely and effectively to support your health and well-being. Whether you're considering starting a new supplement regimen or have questions about your current supplements, consulting with a healthcare professional is a valuable resource for personalized guidance and support.

1. Why are supplements important?

2. What are the different types of supplements?

3. What supplement is good for eye health?

4. How can you make supplements a part of your diet?

5. What role does supplements play in the body?

6. Name 3 Specialized Supplements:

7.Where did Ashwagandha come from?

8.What supplements are essential for heart health?

9.What should you do before adding supplements to your diet? Why?

10. What are some vital supplements our bodies need to function properly?

www.ingramcontent.com/pod-product-compliance
Lightning Source LLC
Chambersburg PA
CBHW071544150726
48000CB00002B/938